Quotations, Context, and Sources: Morton Mintz,
Assisted by Anita Mintz
Why Not the Worst? (Part II): Roberta Mintz
Catalytic Agent and Manager: Daniel Mintz
Design Concept: Margaret Mintz
Research Assistance: Michelle Hall
Advisers: Margaret Mintz, John Birdsall,
and George Lardner, Jr.

ST. MARTIN'S PRESS/NEW YORK

PRESIDENT RON'S APPOINTMENT BOOK

Copyright © 1988 by Father/Daughter Ventures.

Library of Congress Cataloging-in-Publication Data
Mintz, Morton.
  President Ron's appointment book.

  1. Reagan, Ronald—Anecdotes. 2. United States—Politics and government—1981– —Anecdotes, facetiae, satire, etc. 3. United States —Politics and government—1981– —Quotations, maxims, etc.
I. Mintz, Margaret. II. Title.
E877.2.M56 1988 973.927 88-1949
ISBN 0-312-01663-8

Printed in the United States of America

First edition

10 9 8 7 6 5 4 3 2 1

TABLE OF CONTENTS

PART ONE
Stirring Quotations from Reagan's Fanatics,
Finaglers, and Featherheads

PART TWO
Why Not the Worst?

THE RONALD WILSON REAGAN
SCHOOL OF GOVERNMENT

"The way I work is to identify the problem, find the right individuals to do the job, and then let them go to it. I've found this invariably brings out the best in people."
—Address to the Nation, March 4, 1987

". . . the halls of government are as sacred as our temples of worship, and nothing but the highest integrity is required of those who serve in government . . ."
—News conference, April 4, 1984

PART ONE

STIRRING QUOTATIONS FROM REAGAN'S FANATICS, FINAGLERS, AND FEATHERHEADS

■

THE CONFIDENCE MAN

LOUIS O. GIUFFRIDA

Director, Federal Emergency Management Agency
1981–1985

"It [nuclear war] would be a terrible mess, but it wouldn't be unmanageable, to the extent we had a plan."

■

ABC News's *20/20,* April 15, 1982.

THE ECONOMIZERS–I

BILL J. SLOAN
San Francisco Regional Administrator,
Department of Housing and Urban Development
1981–1984

"My wife doesn't like to cook."

■ Sloan proclaimed his deference to Mrs. Sloan on being confronted with evidence that he'd been cooking government books. He'd billed for $6,815 in irregular expenses, mostly in connection with thirty-two weekend visits to his home city of Fresno, California. The expenses included $1,026 for restaurant meals in Fresno, a $31 "dinner," which turned out to be a Disneyland hotel's room-service charge for one bottle of whiskey and two bottles of wine, and $378 for personal phone calls.

Sloan's salary was $63,800. From his office in San Francisco, according to an associate, he was "always sending out letters, urging us not to squander public funds."

Sloan repaid the $6,815 and resigned. He had been a Republican Party official in California before President Reagan appointed him to the HUD post.

■

San Francisco Chronicle, December 17, 1983, and April 11, 1984; Columnist Neal R. Peirce, *Los Angeles Times,* June 25, 1984; and *Washington Post,* April 27, 1986.

THE ECONOMIZERS–II

ROBERT P. NIMMO
Administrator of Veterans Affairs
1981–1982

"What has to be recognized, I think, by [veterans' organizations] if they want to be realistic, is that there are more words in the dictionary than 'more, more, more.' "[1]

■ Nimmo was warning that with millions of World War II veterans soon to reach the age at which they'd be eligible for free medical care from the Veterans Administration the VA may have to limit such care. But having been in office only seven months, Nimmo said, he'd been too busy to decide how to implement a policy of less, less, less.

Later, VA Inspector General Frank S. Sato released the results of a six-week investigation into an allegation by the Better Government Association, an independent government monitor, that Nimmo had used taxpayers' money for personal purposes. Indeed, Sato confirmed, Nimmo had been busy implementing a personal policy of grab, grab, grab.

On June 15, 1982, Nimmo paid the government $5,441 as reimbursement for the wages it had paid to the chauffeur who drove him to and from work—in violation of a 1981 law. He also said he would end a lease under which the government had been paying $708 a month for a Buick Electra—an upgrade from the compacts provided other agency heads. He had spent $54,183 to redecorate his office, adding a shower, and had sent the old furniture

---

[1] Mike Feinsilber, Associated Press, January 10, 1982.

to daughter Mary, a Commerce Department spokesperson.[2]

Meanwhile, the General Accounting Office, the watchdog agency for Congress, found more grab, grab, grab, such as first-class air travel and use of military aircraft. On October 4, 1982—just ahead of the GAO's report—Nimmo resigned. Two other hallmarks of his fourteen months in office: constant criticism from Vietnam veterans for insensitivity to their needs, and unflagging support from Counselor to the President and fellow Californian Edwin Meese III.[3]

THE ECONOMIZERS–III

EDWIN J. GRAY
Chairman, Federal Home Loan Bank Board
1983–1987

"It is not enough to say that travel expense practices at the board during my chairmanship have been virtually identical to long-standing practices of previous . . . boards."

■ The board and its twelve regional Federal Home Loan Banks regulate, audit, and insure savings and loans. The system is funded by assessments levied on the thrifts, which in turn pass on their costs to customers in the form of, e.g., loan charges. But while more and more thrifts were ailing and failing, thrift was of no concern to some

---

[2] *Washington Post,* June 16 and October 5, 1982.
[3] *Washington Post,* December 3, 9, and 11, 1986.

fifty officers of the board and banks who often found it essential to fly to such places as Boca Raton, Hawaii, and Palm Springs. The *Washington Post's* Kathleen Day obtained expense documents in 1986 that told the story. For example:

While on official business in Paris, Gray left his wallet in a phone booth for a few minutes while he sought advice on how to use the phone. When he returned the wallet was gone. The board reimbursed him for the $744 in missing cash and airfare discounts. He became an exceptionally frequent flyer, taking wing for 45,130 reimbursed miles in two months. His wife and daughters live in San Diego, and many of his trips were to San Diego. The entire family and board member Donald I. Hovde attended a three-day meeting in Hawaii, and the banks paid their $2,614 hotel bill.

After another three-day meeting, the board picked up the tab for a cruise on San Francisco Bay ($6,924), for a banquet ($12,324), and for hotel bills for Gray and several other officials. In connection with another meeting, the Atlanta and Indianapolis banks paid $5,856 for their directors' "Dinner Aboard the *Spirit of Charleston.*" The banks spent $9,000 on a celebration when Reagan was inaugurated the second time, and $1,207 on liquor when they welcomed new members of the U.S. League of Savings Institutions, an industry lobby and trade association.

The Office of Government Ethics ruled many board expenses improper. After Day obtained the expense documents and wrote a story, Gray apologized to Congress for "flawed judgments" and ordered officials of the board and banks to end the high living and to accept no more gifts from the industry. His four-year term expired in June 1987.

THE ECONOMIZERS—IV

J. PETER GRACE
Chairman, President's Private Sector Survey on Cost Control in the Federal Government 1982–1984

"Take subsidized bastardy. How many single women with children are there in America? Whatever the precise number, the budget for the Aid to [Families with] Dependent Children program is about $10 billion—So the question is, do you have the right to take money away from hardworking men and women who are earning $20,000 and $30,000 a year and spend it to support all these single women with children? I say you don't."

Interview, The Review of the News, Aug. 26, 1981.

THE SCREENER

ROBERT H. TUTTLE
Deputy Assistant to the President and Director of Presidential Personnel 1985—

"This Administration—has been extraordinarily successful in coming up with people who are extremely well qualified to be ambassadors. They got their jobs because they are qualified and not because they are friends of the President."

■ Peter E. Voss, co-chairman of President Reagan's reelection campaign in Ohio, became chairman of the Postal Service Board of Governors, but coveted an ambassadorship. In early 1986, obliging White House officials chose the Netherlands for him, but the State Department protested that he was unqualified to be our envoy to a country where we have important strategic and trade interests. The White House brushed off the protest and proceeded with its plan to nominate Voss—"until," wrote *Washington Post* reporter John M. Goshko, "it was discovered that Voss had a prior engagement with a federal judge."

In May 1986, Goshko said, "a major probe of Postal Service contracting illegalities resulted in Voss pleading guilty to charges of expense fraud and collecting kickbacks. He was sentenced to four years in prison and fined $11,000.

"Until now, the Administration has managed to keep

Washington Post, April 28, 1987.

quiet the fact that it almost sent a soon-to-be-convicted felon to represent the United States in an important West European capital—

"The Voss case was not an isolated incident. Within days of his guilty plea, the Administration was embarrassed by the forced resignation of William A. Wilson, a political appointee who had been serving as Reagan's emissary to the Vatican. Wilson left after it was revealed that he had engaged in a number of bizarre indiscretions, including a secret 1985 meeting with Libyan leader Moammar Gadhafi at the time the Administration was pressuring its European allies to isolate Libya—Wilson, a former oil company executive and longtime friend of Reagan, repeatedly ignored direct orders from superiors in Washington to break off unauthorized contacts with Libyan officials." (see also The Fabulist–IV.)

■

THE EDUCATOR

DR. EILEEN MARIE GARDNER
Senior Adviser to the Secretary of Education
1985

"There is no injustice in the universe. As unfair as it may seem, a person's external circumstances do fit his level of spiritual development."

╮

■ This generalization about the universe outdid Dr. Gardner, who had been satisfied to find this merely the best of all possible worlds. Gardner wrote it in the draft of a paper in 1983, while she was an analyst for the Heritage Foundation, a conservative think tank and fount of Reaganaut ideology. She also wrote that programs for the handicapped drain resources needed by normal students and are therefore "selfish" and "misguided." Another passage discovered two orders of human development in the universe: a "higher—more advanced—and a lower—less advanced."

Education Secretary William J. Bennett hired Gardner in 1985 to study "educational excellence" in his Office of Education Philosophy and Practice. Soon afterward, while Senator Lowell P. Weicker (R–Conn.) was holding hearings of his Senate Appropriations Subcommittee on Labor, Health, and Human Services, he learned of the paper from Sarah Brady, wife of James S. Brady, the brave White House press secretary. Brady, gravely injured in the head during the attempted assassination of President Reagan, had undergone four years of often excruciating therapy.

At the hearing, Weicker, himself the father of a handicapped child, asked Gardner to explain her paper, but she declined. She did respond to his request for comment about Jim Brady's misfortune. "That is in no way to assume that a person is inferior or bad," she said. "I am saying that what happens to a person in life, the circumstances a person is born into, handicapping conditions, the sex—those circumstances are there to help the person grow toward spiritual perfection."

Gardner resigned the next day.

■

Stephen Engelberg, *New York Times,* April 18, 1985.

THE ALARMIST

GEORGE P. SHULTZ
Secretary of State
1982—

"We'll tell him when he wakes up."

■ At 7 o'clock on a summer morning in 1983, Shultz phoned Speaker Thomas P. O'Neill, Jr., on Cape Cod to report that the Soviets had shot down a Korean airliner—Flight 007. "After telling me what had happened, he said he was sending down a plane to bring me to Washington for an emergency meeting at the White House," O'Neill recalled.

" 'I'll be ready,' I said. 'But what does the President think of this?'

" 'He's still asleep,' said Shultz. " 'He doesn't know about it yet.'

" 'You've got to be kidding,' I said. 'You mean you're calling me before you've even notified the President?'

" 'We'll tell him when he wakes up,' said Shultz. To me, that comment spoke volumes."

■

From *Man of the House: The Life and Political Memoirs of Speaker Tip O'Neill,* by O'Neill and William Novak (New York: Random House, 1987).

THE SHOVELERS–I

DONALD T. REGAN
White House Chief of Staff
1985–1987

"Some of us are like a shovel brigade that follow[s] a parade down Main Street cleaning up."

■ After the 1986 summit meeting with Soviet leader Gorbachev at Reykjavik, President Reagan and his top advisers drew intense criticism for a parade of confusing, conflicting statements on such vital subjects as U.S. official disinformation about Libyan intentions and the growing Iran-contra scandal. More bluntly, the statements were widely perceived as what Vice President George Bush once publicly called "doo-doo." In the ensuing uproar, Regan picked up the shovel to follow the "parade down Main Street" and tried to explain the administration's position to the public.

Regan ran into strong criticism after his statement, because he himself was unschooled in foreign affairs. "I don't take kindly to this criticism by people who have not examined my record," Regan replied. "How much more experience do you have to have in foreign policy than I do to believe you are qualified?"

Regan had had no experience in foreign policy when he came to the White House after a highly successful career on Wall Street, where he had led Merrill Lynch, the giant

Bernard Weinraub, *New York Times,* November 16, 1986.

brokerage firm. The bulls that parade across the television screen in Merrill Lynch commercials are not followed by "doo-doo" shovel brigades.

THE SHOVELERS–II

THOMAS K. JONES

Deputy Undersecretary of Defense for Strategic and Nuclear Forces
1982—

"[In event of a nuclear war,] . . . everybody's going to make it if there are enough shovels to go around. Dig a hole, cover it with a couple of doors, and then throw three feet of dirt on top. It's the dirt that does it."[1]

▪ Jones was one of several administration officials who argued that surviving a nuclear attack would be no different from surviving other major disasters.

Also promoting this cheerfully optimistic view was the Federal Emergency Management Agency, which is in charge of the nation's civil defense program. FEMA offered to newspapers a number of commentaries asserting that "the United States could survive a nuclear attack and go on to recovery within a relatively few years."[2]

---

[1] *Los Angeles Times,* January 22, 1982.
[2] *Los Angeles Times,* January 16, 1982.

THE SHOVELERS–III

CASPAR W. WEINBERGER
Secretary of Defense
1981–1987

"I'd call this a good night's work."[1]

■ In February 1981, David A. Stockman, director of the
Office of Management and Budget, called the Pentagon "a
kind of swamp of $10 to $20 to $30 billion worth of waste
that can be ferreted out if you really push hard."[2] Pushing
with him, he assumed would be the predecessor whose
budget-slashing had won him the title "Cap the Knife."
But Stockman became a pushover for Weinberger and
Frank C. Carlucci, his deputy (and successor), in a half-
hour meeting on January 30, 1981.

Jimmy Carter's military budget was $142 billion in
1980; he proposed "real growth" of 5 percent annually
1981–1986. Reagan wanted 8 or 9 percent, also on the
1980 base. When Weinberger accepted 7 percent, Stockman thought he'd won big. But he'd lost big. Carlucci—
Cap's knife here—suggested 1982 as the base year. Only
after Stockman agreed (later blaming "my horrifying cal-
culator error"), did Weinberger say, "I'd call this a good
night's work."

Some weeks later, Stockman translated the figures into
current dollar values and "nearly had a heart attack. We'd
laid out a plan for a five-year defense budget of 1.46 tril-
lion dollars. . . . Instead of starting from a . . . budget
of $142 billion, we'd started with one of $222 billion. And

---

[1] From David A. Stockman, *The Triumph of Politics: The Inside Story of
the Reagan Revolution* (New York: Avon, 1987).
[2] William Greider, *Atlantic,* December 1981.

by raising that by 7 percent—and compounding it over five years—we had ended up increasing the real growth rate . . . by *10 percent* per year between 1980 and 1986."

Stockman tried to undo his error, but Cap outfoxed him in the Oval Office and at every other major turn. He wrote: "It was ironic in the extreme: the Secretary of Defense of the most tight-fisted and anti-bureaucratic administration of this century had produced a $1.46 trillion budget by delegating the job to the world's largest bureaucracy," where: "The clerks decided what they wanted; the colonels what they wanted; the generals what they wanted . . . and what ended up on the Secretary of Defense's desk was a wish list a mile long." Thus, "Cap the Knife had become Cap the Shovel."[3]

THE RAINMAKER

DAVID A. STOCKMAN
Director, Office of Management and Budget
1981–1985

"Just keep the prevailing winds blowing as they are, and we won't have to worry about it."

■ That was Stockman's invariable (and cynical) comment on acid rain, according to Drew Lewis, who was the Reagan administration's first secretary of transportation. Lewis had become the President's special envoy to Canada in an

---

[3] *The Real David Stockman: The True Story of America's Most Controversial Power Broker,* by John Greenya and Anne Urban (New York: St. Martin's Press, 1983).

effort to resolve sharp differences between the two countries on problems caused by, and responsibilities for, acid rain. In an interview for a highly critical book on Stockman, Lewis referred to the great power Stockman exerted over the public's health, safety, and most every other function of the federal government:

"I think he was very political and very devious . . . What you'd you find with Stockman in these budget presentations was that he would have put together about two-thirds of the facts, and he would make a very convincing argument, but you'd never hear the other third—I think he manipulated the statistics to the extent that he used the ones that proved his point, and he never got to the ones that proved the opposite point."

Lewis said of Stockman: "When you'd catch him in something that was obviously misleading or a falsehood or whatever you want to call it, he would [react] with great indignation until you'd fully documented that you'd caught him, and then he'd say, 'Fine.' I never thought he was particularly arrogant. Take, for example, acid rain. He was not too pleased when I got that assignment on acid rain. His explanation *[sic]* on acid rain had always been, 'Just keep the prevailing winds blowing . . .' "

THE OPTIMIST

DONALD P. HODEL
Secretary of the Interior
1985—

"People who don't stand out in the sun—it [ultraviolet radiation] doesn't affect them."[1]

■ Thus did Hodel address the massive health implications of the dramatic erosion of the ozone layer, the earth's natural shield against ultraviolet rays. These can cause human skin cancer and damage crops and marine life. The greatest erosion of the layer has been caused by cholorfluorocarbons, which are most widely used as coolants in refrigerators and air conditioners.

A worldwide campaign has been building for global controls on the chemicals. But in May 1987, reports surfaced of discussions in the administration in which some senior officials played down the dangers of ultraviolet radiation. They suggested that individuals could protect themselves against cancer and other diseases caused by the rays by wearing protective gear, such as hats and sunglasses. One official said that skin cancer induced by radiation is a "self-inflicted disease."

Despite these views, the United States became on September 16, 1987, one of twenty-four signatories to an agreement to protect the ozone layer. The pact, the first multinational treaty to restrict air pollutants, will take ef-

---

[1] Robert E. Taylor, *Wall Street Journal,* May 29, 1987.

fect as soon as it is signed by eleven countries in which at least two-thirds of the world's chlorofluorocarbons are consumed.[2]

■

THE DEVILS' ADVOCATE

FREDRIC N. ANDRE
Commissioner, the Interstate Commerce Commission
1982—

"Bribes among principals are probably one of the clearest instances of the free market at work . . .

"Well, they are just discounts . . . A bribe is a rebate, is it not? . . . It is an attempt to get around the rigidities imposed on the market by a government cartel."

"I think murderers in jail, there is no reason why—if the general cultural laws of this country permit them to run trucking companies—they are in jail because they are a physical danger to other people, but that does not mean their mind is utterly corrupt as far as running a surface transportation business is concerned . . .

"Think of all the businessmen . . . who still

---

[2] *Facts on File,* September 18, 1987.

run their companies from jail . . . Why should we have a higher standard, of all things, in surface transportation?"

"No one has yet proven that a monopoly price that came about as a result purely of market activity has ever been socially onerous."

■ Andre seized the moral high ground on October 20, 1982, when the commissioners swapped ideas about what should be the nature of ICC oversight of a trucking industry that Congress was largely freeing from decades of regulation. The meeting was closed, and the commissioners did not expect what they said to be quoted; but the Transportation Consumer Action Project, founded by Ralph Nader, obtained the transcript under the Freedom of Information Act and released it.

Other commissioners, in what one called "a philosophical discussion," tried to apply the brakes to the free-wheeling Andre, a one-time truck driver. For example, Chairman Reese H. Taylor, Jr., also a Reagan appointee, said "I can't agree" that bribes show a free market is thriving.

Andre, then forty-nine, was a deputy commissioner of the Indiana Bureau of Motor Vehicles before joining the Reagan transition team and then, in March 1982, the ICC.

■

Howard Kurtz and Douglas B Feaver, *Washington Post,* December 18, 1982.

THE INSIDE DOPESTER–I

GEORGE H. BUSH
Vice President of the United States
1981—

"I'm in on everything. If our policies aren't working, I can't say, 'Wait a minute, I'm not to blame . . . I feel I'm a full partner.' "[1]

■ Later, David S. Broder interviewed Bush, who, ". . . asserting his truthfulness had been vindicated in the Iran-contra hearings, said . . . his judgment in the affair cannot be fairly criticized by 1988 presidential campaign opponents because he had been 'denied information' about what was going on.

". . . Bush said he had not advised the President against selling arms to Iran, in part because he never heard strong objections to that policy. 'If I'd have sat there and heard Secretary of State George Shultz and Cap (Defense Secretary Casper) Weinberger express it [opposition] strongly,' he said, 'maybe I would have had a stronger view. But when you don't know something, it's hard to react . . . We were not in the loop . . .' "

Four months after the interview, the Senate Iran-contra panel released a Poindexter note telling of Bush's "solid" support of the arms-for-hostages deal.[2] Three weeks after that, Bob Woodward and Walter Pincus of the *Washington Post* all but demolished Bush's "not in the loop" claim:

"Vice President Bush watched the secret arms sale to Iran unfold step by step and was more informed of details

---

[1] Interview with Richard Fly, *Business Week,* August 18, 1986.
[2] *Washington Post,* August 6 and December 18, 1987.

than he has acknowledged because of his regular attendance at President Reagan's morning national security briefings and other meetings, according to his statements to the Tower commission, other Iran-contra documents and interviews with former administration officials."[3]

■

THE INSIDE DOPESTER–II

GEORGE H. BUSH
Vice President of the United States
1981—

"We love your adherence to democratic principles and democratic processes."[1]

■ Thus did Bush toast Ferdinand Marcos during inaugural festivities for the Philippine president in Manila. Later, Bush reaffirmed his admiration for the corrupt, ruthless dictator. Bush told a news conference in Honolulu:

"I'll repeat it and stand by it . . . We should judge by the record."[1]

■ The record of the Marcos regime is thoroughly familiar to William Chapman, a former foreign correspondent who has reported on the Philippines for years. He wrote in his 1987 book: "Virtually every democratic institution erected

---

[3] *Washington Post,* January 7, 1988.
[1] Lindy Washburn, Associated Press, July 2, 1981.

since independence was attained in 1946 was dismantled: the Congress, political parties, the free and lively press, the independent judiciary. The American 'showcase of democracy' in Asia was smashed."[2]

■

THE INSIDE DOPESTER–III

GEORGE H. BUSH
Vice President of the United States
1981—

"It's the only memorable thing I've ever said, and I've regretted saying it."[1]

■ The "memorable thing" was Bush's description of Ronald Reagan's proposal to cut individual taxes 30 percent across the board (while increasing military spending and balancing the budget): "voodoo economics."

Bush committed this truth while campaigning for the Republican presidential campaign nomination in 1980. A few months later, after Reagan had won the nomination and picked Bush as his running mate, Bush muttered audibly into a microphone during a debate in Baltimore: "God, I wish I hadn't said that."[2]

Actually, Bush was being too modest. Here's another memorable thing he said:

---

[2] *Inside the Philippine Revolution* (New York: Norton, 1987).
[1] November 30, 1987.
[2] *Washington Post,* September 23, 1980.

"Hey, when the mechanics who keep those tanks running run out of work in the Soviet Union, send them to Detroit because we could use that kind of ability."

■ Bush said this at a meeting of NATO ambassadors in Brussels after learning of a Soviet military operation in which none of 350 tanks had broken down.

Not surprisingly, the remark was damaging to the V.P.'s presidential campaign. Bush issued a full, unhesitating apology.[3]

■

THE DRUG COMPANY ADDICT

GEORGE H. BUSH
Vice President of the United States and Chairman of the President's Task Force on Regulatory Relief
1981—

"I think we've started to see . . . the end, or the beginning of the end of this adversary relationship. Government shouldn't be an adversary. It ought to be a partner."[1]

---

[3] David Hoffman, *Washington Post,* October 3, 1987
[1] Speech to the International Federation of Pharmaceutical Manufacturers Associations, Washington, D.C., June 7, 1982.

■ Bush wanted to make pharmaceutical manufacturers a partner of the Food and Drug Administration. He had been a director of one of the largest would-be partners, Eli Lilly and Company, from 1977 to 1979, when he began his campaign for the Republican presidential nomination. Lilly's general counsel was Indiana's member of the Bush campaign steering committee.

When Bush assumed the Vice Presidency in 1981, he held $145,000 worth of drug stocks including 1,500 shares of Lilly. Since then he has either sold the stocks or placed them in blind trust.

Three months before proposing the partnership, Bush wrote to Treasury Secretary Donald Regan to urge Treasury to alter plans to modify a provision of the tax law that had enabled drug companies—including Lilly—to avoid billions of dollars of taxes on income earned in Puerto Rico. Later, Bush disengaged, saying he felt "uncomfortable about the appearance of my active, personal involvement in the details of a tax matter directly affecting a company with which I once had a close association."[2]

In 1985, Lilly pleaded guilty to twenty-five criminal charges of failing to notify the FDA of numerous deaths among overseas users of Oraflex, an arthritis drug. Lilly knew of the deaths before the FDA approved the drug for sale in this country. Despite such criminal prosecutions of drug companies, Bush continued into 1987 to try to weaken FDA regulation of the industry.[3]

■

[2] *New York Times,* May 19, 1982.
[3] *Washington Post,* August 22, 1985, and July 15, 1987.

THE GIRLS' BEST FRIEND

DONALD T. REGAN

White House Chief of Staff

1985–1987

"Are the women of America prepared to give up their jewelry?"[1]

■ In defending the Reagan administration's opposition to the imposition of sanctions on South Africa, this White House diamond in the rough was suggesting that American women of course prefer more baubles to an end to apartheid. This was more ebullient bull than bullion. Regan had no basis for gratuitously presuming that American women lacked compassion and intelligence. His question had the familiar, condescending ring of an earlier compliment Regan had paid to women:

"They're [women] not . . . going to understand throw-weights, or what is happening in Afghanistan or what is happening in human rights. Some women will, but most women—

---

[1] Regan made this remark to the *Baltimore Sun* and *Chicago Tribune* on background, meaning they weren't allowed to name the senior official who made it. After their stories appeared on July 17, 1986, however, other White House officials identified Regan as the source.

believe me for the most part if you took a poll—
would rather read the human interest stuff of
what happened."[2]

THE FABULIST–I

WILLIAM F. BAXTER
Assistant Attorney General, Antitrust Division,
Department of Justice
1981–1983

"No one in his right mind could possibly
suppose there was a connection between the
concentration of economic markets and political
power."[1]

---

[2] *Washington Post,* November 18, 1985. Reporter Donnie Radcliffe
interviewed Regan at the Reagan-Gorbachev summit in Geneva.
[1] *New York Times,* March 29, 1982.

THE FABULISTS–II

ERNEST W. LEFEVER

Nominee, Assistant Secretary of State for Human Rights and Humanitarian Affairs
1981

"My pious Protestant parents taught me that serving humanity was the highest earthly good . . ."[1]

Nestle, S.A., the giant Swiss food conglomerate, became the world's largest seller of infant formula, partly by luring Third World women to abandon breast milk—the nearly perfect food—for costly formula, which often could be prepared only with impure water in unclean bottles.

A coalition of religious and other groups organized a global boycott. Nestle countered with covert operations. In one, it slipped $25,000 to the Ethics and Public Policy Center, a tax-exempt foundation founded and led by Ernest Lefever.

He commissioned a (never-completed) study that led to a *Fortune* article calling religious boycotters "Marxists marching under the banner of Christ." Lefever then changed the title (without permission) to "Crusade Against the Corporation: Churches and the Nestle Boycott," and sent out reprints. "I am not influenced by the source of contributions," he said.[2]

---

[1] Lefever's autobiographical entry in *Who's Who in America*.
[2] Morton Mintz, *Washington Post,* January 4, 1981.

In 1981, President Reagan picked Lefever for the human rights post. At his confirmation hearing, the Senate Foreign Relations Committee pried out of him these admissions: Nestle had contributed $5,000 just in time for the EPPC to pay out $5,000 to start the study, and the $20,000 balance in the nick of time for a large mailing to a list of community leaders provided by a public relations firm. The "friend" who had referred him to the PR firm was Thomas J. Ward, Nestle's Washington lawyer,[3] himself a secret $10,000 donor.[4]

Lefever swore that "we didn't do anything to please Nestle," and that "Nestle had nothing to do" with reprinting and distributing the *Fortune* article. Then Henry Ciocca, former director of corporate responsibility for Nestle, said the EPPC had taken Nestle funds for that very purpose. Finally, Lefever admitted having asked Nestle to fund the study. The Senate committee voted him down, 13 to 4.[4]

[3] John M. Goshko and Scott Armstrong, *Washington Post,* May 19, 1981
[4] Armstrong, *Washington Post,* May 22 and June 7, 1981.

THE FABULISTS–III

RICHARD V. ALLEN
*Assistant to the President
for National Security Affairs
1981–1982*

"My connections have nothing to do with my business activism."[1]

■ So Allen swore at the perjury trial of Michael K. Deaver, former deputy chief of staff to President Reagan. Many reporters choked on the claim, having revealed numerous examples of Allen's long-standing inability, as the *Wall Street Journal's* Jonathan Kwitny put it, "to distinguish between the affairs of government and his own personal business interests."[2]

Well before the Reagan Presidency, Kwitny and others had documented numerous examples of Allen's questionable government-related dealings.[3] One of Kwitny's examples follows:

"On July 31, 1972, Mr. Allen left his full-time job as deputy assistant to the President [Nixon] for international economic affairs. Within a month he negotiated a $60,000-a-year-plus-expenses job with the Overseas Companies of Portugal, to become a Washington advocate of white colonial rule in Africa. (At the time, Angola and Mozambique were still colonies of Portugal.) Mr. Allen filed with the

---

[1] *New Republic,* November 30, 1987.
[2] *Wall Street Journal,* October 28, 1980.
[3] *Mother Jones,* September/October 1980; *Washington Post,* October 30, 1980.

Justice Department as a foreign agent on May 13 of the following year.

"In the meantime, for 11 months after leaving government service, Mr. Allen remained on the government's roster as a per diem consultant, according to White House personnel records. Mr. Allen vigorously denies that he was ever employed by the government during this period . . ."

In November 1981 Allen was revealed to have taken from Japanese journalists $1,000 meant as an honorarium for Nancy Reagan. The ensuing mini-scandal led him to resign in January 1982, but the Justice Department cleared him of any crime. By mid-1983, he was, among other things, a consultant, at $300,000 a year, "for a consortium of Japanese firms favoring construction of a second Panama Canal."[4]

■

THE FABULISTS–IV

FAITH RYAN WHITTLESEY
Ambassador to Switzerland
1981–1983, 1985—

"I had no role in it."

■ A House Foreign Affairs subcommittee called a hearing to ask Whittlesey to explain her bizarre personnel practices at the embassy. For example, she booted out a career Foreign Service officer to hire—at $62,400—the right wing son of a man who had given $5,000 to her $80,000 "rep-

---

[4] *Newsweek,* June 6, 1983.

resentational" fund, which she used to entertain luminaries, such as Attorney General Edwin Meese, III, and Teamsters President Jackie Presser, and to buy sundry items, including $15,000 worth of silver serving pieces, and $1,000 worth of Christmas cards graced by her picture.[1]

While Assistant to the President for Public Liaison from 1983 to 1985, Whittlesey had worked closely with Lieutenant Colonel Oliver L. North. In 1986, when her conduct in Bern led to a Justice Department probe, North offered to find her a lawyer.[1] Columnist Mary McGrory called the pair "missionaries for the contra cause; he, raising millions, dispatching planes, browbeating Latin-American leaders; she . . . importing speakers to rouse private groups to a pitch of zeal equal to her own."[2]

At the hearing, McGrory wrote, Whittlesey "responded readily and with some hauteur to everything but questions from Rep. Chester G. Atkins (D–Mass.), who seemed to be in the grip of a suspicion that Whittlesey had gone to Bern to establish another base of contra support. He inquired about the two-week delay in forwarding to the Swiss government the [Justice Department's] request to freeze the funds in North's secret bank accounts.

"I had no role in it," she said.

"Did you or your staff engage in communications with the NSC regarding the delay in filing the freeze request?"

"For the first time in the long afternoon, Whittlesey paused," McGrory wrote. "She looked at her lawyer. She said she knew only what the legal attaché told her."[2]

---

[1] Howard Kurtz, *Washington Post*, September 26 and 27, October 3 and 11, and December 6, 1986, and March 11, 1987.
[2] *Washington Post*, March 12, 1987.

THE ORDER TAKER

LIEUTENANT-COLONEL OLIVER L. NORTH

Deputy Director of the Political-Military Affairs Bureau, National Security Council 1981–1986

"I never carried out a single act, not one, in which I did not have authority from my superiors. I haven't in the 23 years that I have been in the uniformed services of the United States of America ever violated an order, not one."[1]

■ North's testimony referred to acts he had carried out as the chief executor of a program in which U.S. arms were illegally sold to Iran and profits from the sale diverted to the Nicaraguan Contras. He also helped set up and run a covert operation to send weapons and provisions to the Contras during a period in which U.S. aid was restricted.

Senator Daniel K. Inouye (D–Hawaii), chairman of the Senate Iran-contra committee, responded pointedly to North's assertion that he was only following orders. North, Inouye noted, was subject to the Uniform Code of Military Justice. "And that code makes it abundantly clear that orders of a superior officer must be obeyed by subordinate members, but it is lawful orders," Inouye stressed. "In fact, it says, members of the military have an obligation to disobey unlawful orders."[2]

---

[1] Testimony before the congressional Iran-contra committees, July, 1987.
[2] *Washington Post,* July 14, 1987.

North and his boss, Rear Admiral John M. Poindexter (see The Government unto Himself), shared the 1987 "Doublespeak Award." North won because he "never called any of his actions lying," said Professor William Lutz of Rutgers University, chairman of the Committee on Public Doublespeak of the National Council of Teachers of English.[3]

■

THE ROBIN HOOD (IN THE IRANIAN FOREST)

LIEUTENANT-COLONEL OLIVER L. NORTH

Deputy Director of the Political-Military Affairs Bureau National Security Council 1981–1986

"And I still to this day, Counsel, don't see anything wrong with taking the Ayatollah's money and sending it to support the Nicaraguan freedom fighters."

■ What he affected not to see as "wrong" was this: the Ayatollah was taking our weapons to use against Iraq, in violation of President Reagan's assurances to the American public, our European allies, and the Middle East countries that justly fear Iran. The resulting damage to U.S. credibility, particularly as a bulwark of the interna-

---

[3] *Parade,* January 10, 1988.
Washington Post, June 8, 1987.

tional alliance against terrorism, was incalculable. Not to mention the preponderance of evidence that the dealings with the contras constituted a flagrant violation of the Boland amendment.

■

THE LOYALISTS–I

ELLIOTT ABRAMS
Assistant Secretary of State
1985—

"We have not received a dime from a foreign government."

■ When Abrams testified before the Senate Intelligence Committee on November 25, 1986, he spoke a narrow truth, so far as is known: no one in the U.S. government had received money from another nation for the contra cause. Not yet. Not quite. However, a year earlier, on the authority of Secretary of State George P. Shultz, Abrams himself had traveled to London, to meet an emissary from Brunei. In London, in a rendezvous in a park, Abrams identified himself to the representative as a "Mr. Kenilworth," and suggested that in exchange for a $10 million contribution to the contras, Brunei would earn the "gratitude" of the American President and secretary of state. In his 1986 testimony, Abrams did not mention this meeting.

Later, on June 25, 1987, when Abrams testified before Congress again, he admitted he had been evasive in the earlier hearing. Representative Jim Moody (D–Wis.) char-

Washington Post, June 26, 1987.

acterized Abrams's testimony: "You had to be a Philadelphia lawyer in pinning down Abrams. In answering questions, he answered them in the most narrow, misleading way."

Angered by Abrams's deception, 129 House Democrats signed a letter to Schultz demanding that Abrams either "resign or be replaced immediately" . . . because he "knowingly and deliberately misled Congress" and "can no longer function effectively."

Secretary Shultz responded by praising Abrams for "doing a sensational job," and defending the falsehood: "We had given that country (Brunei] a pledge of absolute confidentiality and Mr. Abrams properly felt bound by that pledge."

THE LOYALISTS—II

ROBERT C. McFARLANE
National Security Adviser to the President
1983–1985

"I can state with deep personal conviction that at no time did I or any member of the National Security Council staff violate the letter or the spirit of the law."

"We did not solicit funds or other support for military or paramilitary activities either from Americans or third parties."

"There is no official or unofficial relationship with any member of the NSC staff regarding fund-raising for the Nicaraguan democratic opposition."[1]

■ Less than two years after making these claims, McFarlane, who had himself gone to Iran (with a cake and a Bible) in pursuit of the arms-for-hostages deal, testified at the congressional Iran-contra hearings:

. "The President had made clear that he wanted a job done."[2]

■ This exchange followed:
   Q. "Earlier today, in extended testimony, you indicated that the assurances you gave to the Congress, in your letters about contra activity, were, to say the least, overstated."
   A. "I think that's true."[3]

■

---

[1] Letters to Rep. Lee H. Hamilton (D–Ind.) in August, September, and October 1985.
[2] May 11, 1987
[3] May 12, 1987.

THE GOVERNMENT UNTO HIMSELF

REAR ADMIRAL JOHN M. POINDEXTER
National Security Adviser to the President 1985–1986

"I simply didn't want any outside interference."[1]

■ This was Poindexter's response to a fundamental question put by House counsel John W. Nields, Jr. during the Iran-contra hearings: What was "the real reason to withhold information from Congress" about the funneling of funds from the sale of arms to Iran to the contras? His candor—if that is what it was—was irrevocably stained by its revelation of a gross disregard for the democratic safeguards of "outside interference" against one-man rule.

Poindexter and Lieutenant Colonel Oliver L. North shared the 1987 "Doublespeak Award," conferred by the Committee on Public Doublespeak of the National Council of Teachers of English. Committee Chairman William Lutz found Poindexter's testimony cluttered with doublespeak, such as calling the transfer of millions of taxpayers' dollars a "technical implementation" done without a "substantive decision."[2]

■

---

[1] Testimony before the Congressional Iran-contra hearings, July 15, 1987.
[2] *Parade,* January 10, 1988.

THE INSULATOR

REAR ADMIRAL JOHN M. POINDEXTER
National Security Adviser to the President
1985–1986

". . . So although I was convinced that we could properly do it and that the President would approve if asked, I made a very deliberate decision not to ask the President so that I could insulate him from the decision and provide some future deniability for the President if it ever leaked out. Of course, our hope was that it would not leak out."[1]

■ Some thought Poindexter was stepping into a prearranged role of "fall guy" when he assumed ultimate responsibility for the diversion to the contras of proceeds from the sale of arms to Iran. However, as national security adviser, he had a constituency of one to whom he was accountable: the President.

Even after the White House issued a statement disagreeing with Poindexter's assertion, he insisted throughout his testimony that, had Ronald Reagan known of the diversion, he would have approved it.

■

---

[1] Testimony before the congressional Iran-contra hearings, July 14, 1987.

THE ETHICIST

PATRICK J. BUCHANAN
Assistant to the President and Director of White House Communications
1985–1987

"For all this moralizing that 'the end does not justify the means,' the truth is the colonel's ends were noble and his means—secrecy and shredding documents—licit or not, were not inherently immoral."[1]

■ In Buchanan's angelology, North is on the side of the blessed spirits and those who are not gripped by anticommunism are among the demons. Thus, in a signed article headlined "Whom Will History Indict?" Buchanan weighed the legislative actions of the Democratically controlled Congress against the deeds of Colonel North, and found the lawmakers wanting:

"Indeed, with its Clark amendment cutting off aid to the pro-Western guerrillas in Angola, and its Boland amendments cutting off aid to the pro-American guerrillas in Nicaragua, the liberal wing of the Democratic Party has made itself the silent partner—the indispensable ally—of revolutionary communism in the Third World . . . If Nicaragua has now been made safe for communism and the Warsaw Pact, history will hold the part of O'Neill

---

[1] *Washington Post*, July 19, 1987.

and Foley and Wright fully answerable and accountable. What crime has Ollie North ever committed—to
rival that?"[2]

■

THE INVESTIGATOR

BRETTON G. SCIARONI
General Counsel, Intelligence Oversight Board
1984–1987

"Well, my investigation was probably as
thorough as the one that had been conducted by
the Hill [Congress]."

■ The Intelligence Advisory Board has three unpaid members and one lawyer, Sciaroni. He failed bar exams twice
in California and twice in the District of Colombia before
passing one in Pennsylvania, where he has never lived or
practiced. His success the fifth time around enabled him
to practice in the District, and his first job as an attorney
—at $62,000 a year—was with the little-known IOB. The
IOB was created by President Ford in 1976 after disclosures that intelligence agencies had engaged in illegal conduct.

Although the IOB's mission is to check into possible
illegalities by spy agencies, not to advise them, Sciaroni
confirmed at a hearing of the congressional Iran-contra
committees that in April 1985 he had sent Lieutenant

---

[2] *Newsweek,* July 13, 1987.
Charles R. Babcock, *Washington Post,* June 9, 1987.

Colonel Oliver L. North, the National Security Council staff aide, a draft legal opinion on "the legal basis for covert action in Central America." In an attached note, he asked North to "give me your comments (at your leisure of course). Thanks."

In August 1985 Sciaroni read allegations in news accounts that North had violated the Boland amendment's ban on aid to the contras. His investigation, he testified, consisted of a quick document review, a five-minute chat with North, and a thirty-minute talk with an NSC staff attorney, Commander Paul B. Thompson. North and Thompson assured him the allegations were false, and he wrote a legal opinion that the Boland ban didn't cover the NSC.

■

THE GOOD RIDDER OF BAD RUBBISH

JAMES B. EDWARDS
Secretary of Energy
1981–1982

"Thank God we have these nuclear wastes because if we didn't we would probably all be working in salt mines in Siberia today and we would not be worried about nuclear waste."[1]

■ Edwards, then governor of South Carolina and chairman

---

[1] Hearing of the House Subcommittee on Fossil and Nuclear Energy, June 20, 1978.

of the National Governors Association's nuclear energy subcommittee, had been asked if his fellow South Carolinians would allow a nuclear repository in their state. He made the above response after saying that the state had already become a repository for "millions of gallons of defense waste."

Edwards is a dentist and nuclear-energy enthusiast whose ache to fill cavities extended to radioactive waste. At the confirmation hearing, held by the Energy and Natural Resources Subcommittee of the Senate Commerce Committee, Senator Dale Bumpers (D–Ark.) asked the nominee, "What does 'Three Mile Island' conjure up in your mind?"

"It conjures up a company that's in trouble and needs some help."[2]

[2] *Science* magazine, February 6, 1981.

THE FOXES WHO GUARDED THE CHICKEN COOPS–I

EDWARD L. ROWNY

Special Representative for Arms Control
and Disarmament Negotiations
1981–1985
Senior Presidential Arms Control Adviser
1985–

". . . we have put too much emphasis on the control of arms and too little on the provision of arms."[1]

■ This conclusion, Rowny said, stemmed from his six and a half years with SALT (Strategic Arms Limitation Talks). Under Presidents Nixon, Ford, and Carter, Rowny was the Joint Chiefs of Staff representative to SALT. In 1979, he retired from the Army in order to oppose the SALT II treaty, which, he claimed, would put the United States in a strategic position inferior to that of the Soviet Union. Nonetheless, the treaty was signed in the same year.[2]

It goes without saying that Rowny's hostility to arms control was seen by President Reagan and such hardliners as Secretary of Defense Caspar W. Weinberger and Assistant Secretary of Defense Richard N. Perle, as a splendid credential. So, in 1981, the retired lieutenant general was anointed Special Representative for Arms Control, with

---

[1] Statement made at the National Defense University in 1980. Quoted in Ronald Brownstein and Nina Easton, *Reagan's Ruling Class* (New York: Pantheon, 1983).
[2] *New York Times,* May 1, 1981; June 30, 1982; and October 19, 1987.

the rank of ambassador, and, in 1982, went to Geneva to begin to negotiate with the Soviet Union a new treaty on reductions in long-range nuclear weapons.

In December 1987, after both Weinberger and Perle left the Pentagon, a thawed Reagan signed a treaty with the Soviet Union to eliminate medium-range missiles in Europe. Rowny had said in May 1987 that if such a treaty failed to satisfy his concerns about verification, he might oppose ratification. But in October he wrote guardedly: "The final agreement will be a significant political and diplomatic accomplishment." Citing the imbalances in conventional forces and strategic arms, he concluded, "We are only at the beginning of the task of reducing the Soviet military threat."[2]

THE FOXES WHO GUARDED THE CHICKEN COOPS–II

ERNEST W. LEFEVER

Nominee, Assistant Secretary of State for Human Rights and Humanitarian Affairs
1981

"In a formal, a legal sense, the U.S. government has no responsibility—and certainly no authority—to promote human rights in other sovereign states."[1]

---

[1] Associated Press, May 10, 1981. The nomination was defeated. (See The Fabulists–II on pages 32–33.)

THE FOXES WHO GUARDED THE CHICKEN COOPS–III

DREW LEWIS
Secretary of Transportation
1981–1983

"If I could do it, there would be a four-year moratorium [on new regulations]."[1]

■ Perhaps the most important of such regulations, concerning auto safety, had already been postponed for fifteen years. Yet, wrote Joan Claybrook, who headed the National Highway Traffic Safety Administration under President Carter, "Every 10 minutes, 24 hours a day, 365 days a year, another American is killed in a motor vehicle crash, and every 10 seconds another person is injured." Air bags would radically reduce this toll. Each year they would enable an estimated 6,400 persons to survive frontal crashes, and 120,000 more to have minor, rather than moderate to critical injuries. By 1984, air bags had become the most tested vehicle-safety device: a billion miles of actual road use and 5,000 crash tests.[2]

A ruling, Safety Standard 208, to require air bags, or other passive restraints, was first proposed in 1969. During the following eight years, 208 was issued, delayed, and rescinded. Then, in 1977, Secretary Brock Adams revived it, but gave the industry four to six years to comply.

Ronald Reagan's election changed all that. Lewis and

---

[1] *Washington Star,* February 11, 1981, quoting a Lewis speech to the National Automobile Dealers Association.
[2] Joan Claybrook and the staff of Public Citizen, *Retreat from Safety: Reagan's Attack on America's Health.* (New York: Pantheon, 1984).

Vice President George H. Bush, guided by an agenda prepared by General Motors, Ford, and Chrysler, called for thirty-four actions to help the U.S auto industry, including relaxation of 208 and other crash-protection standards. Lewis proposed delaying 208 in February 1981 and killed it outright eight months later.

In 1982, the insurance industry and consumer groups challenged Lewis's action. A federal appeals court agreed with them and ruled against DOT for failing to "heed the goals that Congress asked it to meet." DOT appealed, but in 1983, after Lewis had resigned, a presumptively friendly Supreme Court upheld the appeals court—unanimously.

By 1990, twenty-four years after Congress's mandate, all new cars will be required to have air bags or other automatic restraints for the driver. Front-seat passengers will have to wait until 1994. Had Lewis let 208 stand, we would have had air bags in 1984.

■

THE FOXES WHO GUARDED THE CHICKEN COOPS–IV

RAYMOND PECK
Administrator, National Highway Traffic Safety Administration
1981–1983

For Ronald Reagan, Peck, a lawyer for the coal industry with no visible knowledge of, or sympathy for, safety and health programs of any kind, was a Mercedes Benz of a choice to run the NHTSA, and to pull the trigger when Drew Lewis, Secretary of Transportation, shot Safety Standard 208 for air bags. Representative Timothy E.

Wirth (D–Colo.), chairman of a House Energy and Commerce subcommittee, had this exchange with Peck:

Q. "What are you doing for safety?"

A. "Let me give you a specific example."

Q. "That is what I want . . ."

A. "One. We have approved an internal order to assure that petitions for rulemaking are classified within seven days, handled within 30 days, and depending upon the actual complexity of the issue, finally resolved."

Q. "Let us [not] talk about . . . internal bureaucracy at NHTSA. What are you doing [for] safety on the highways?"

A. "Mr. Chairman, this is the heart of our rulemaking responsibilities . . ."

Q. "I would like to know for the record, right now, what have you done? . . . I have gotten no response yet in terms of what this administration has done about highway safety . . ."

A. "Now, Mr. Chairman, that is neither a fair nor an appropriate question."

Q. "I cited the start, the intent and the purpose of [the National Traffic and Motor Vehicle Safety Act of 1966] '. . . To reduce traffic accidents and deaths and injuries . . . resulting from traffic accidents.' "

A. ". . . I have found that the 208 [air bag] standard would not have led to highway safety . . ."

Q. "I hear, already, what you are not doing, all right. What I would like to know again, if I could re-pose the question, all right, is what you are doing for safety?"

A. "Mr. Chairman, I have already introduced into the record the three management processes whereby we will make research and development priority decisions, rulemaking priority decisions and rulemaking evaluation decisions. Those documents . . . fully answer your questions."

■

THE FOXES WHO GUARDED THE CHICKEN COOPS–V

RAYMOND BARNHART
Administrator, the Federal Highway Administration
1981–

"I think it's a stinking law, but I'm going to enforce it."

■ The law he had taken an oath to enforce, presumably

Telecommunications, Consumer Protection, and Finance Subcommittee hearing, March 23, 1982.
Associated Press, May 10, 1981.

while holding his nose, set the highway speed limit at fifty-five miles per hour. It was one of a number of matters that Barnhart, as highway chief in Texas, had quarreled about with the Department of Transportation. Thus may he have earned, in the eyes of the President Reagan, a top job at DOT.

In Texas, Barnhart had also scented his appeal to the new administration by attacking the federal rules that require the award to minority contractors of a certain proportion of the subcontracts on federal projects.

"When the feds say you must subcontract out a percentage of your work to minorities, ethnics and women, it is unconscionable."

∎

THE FOXES WHO GUARDED THE CHICKEN COOPS–VI

LANDO W. ZECH, JR.
Chairman, the Nuclear Regulatory Commission 1986–

Nearly one in ten U.S. nuclear plants is shut down for safety reasons, and

"Surely that is evidence that we are a tough regulator."

Cass Peterson, *Washington Post,* December 21, 1987.

This non sequitur was Zech's spin on a report in which the House Interior and Insular Affairs investigations subcommittee, after a six-month probe, accused the NRC of an "unhealthy empathy" for the nuclear industry, and of a zealotry for nuclear power that compromised public safety and health. "On a number of occasions, the NRC has acted as if it were the advocate for, and not the regulator of, the nuclear industry," the report said. Here are examples:

*What the NRC called an "alarming increase" in drug-related safety incidents at nuclear plants was met by the agency in 1986 with a policy statement—one that didn't provide for penalties for violations.

*NRC inspectors who found evidence of drug problems at a plant gave the evidence to the operators. Instead of the remedial action that is supposed to follow under the NRC's theory of self-regulation, the operators ordered an in-house investigation—by an employee who was later arrested for possession of drugs.

*In 1980, after a near-disaster at the Tennessee Valley Authority's Browns Ferry plant in Alabama, the NRC issued a rule intended to prevent fires from disabling safety gear. In 1985—over the protests of agency fire experts, and with no public notice—the NRC wrote an "interpretation" of the rule that essentially let plant operators decide for themselves what fire-safety standards to obey.

The report, as had Subcommittee Chairman Sam Gejdenson (D–Conn.) and five other congressional committee heads, urged President Reagan to fire Commissioner Thomas M. Roberts (see next page). The report also accused Roberts of meddling in an Office of Government Ethics investigation into conflict-of-interest allegations against the TVA's nuclear manager. Roberts called the report "neither fair nor accurate."

THE FOXES WHO GUARDED THE CHICKEN COOPS–VII

THOMAS M. ROBERTS
Commissioner, the Nuclear Regulatory Commission
1984–

"I continue to respect and honor the public trust that has been placed in me."[1]

■ In connection with serious safety defects at the Waterford Nuclear Plant, a confidential NRC staff memo cited "possible collusion" between the agency and the plant operator, Louisiana Power and Light Company. In 1985 in Memphis—Roberts's home city—NRC inspectors searched the files of Middle South Services, which owns the utility. They found not only the memo, but also a note in which a Middle South vice president urged its concealment "to protect the source within the NRC." Both documents bore the initials of Roberts, whom President Reagan had named to a second six-year term.

Middle South's possession of the memo gave it "a tremendous advantage" in coping with a subsequent NRC probe, Ben Hayes, chief of the agency's Office of Investigations, told the Senate Governmental Affairs Committee in 1987. He also testified that the leak had never been fully investigated, and that his bosses had ordered him to give all of his notes to Roberts.

Roberts testified he'd tried to ferret out the leaker, but, failing, had destroyed Hayes's notes. These, said Committee Chairman John H. Glenn, Jr. (D–Ohio), were "incrim-

---

[1] Associated Press, June 20, 1987.

inating evidence." Roberts, motivated to search his files anew, found the memo and the notes and sent them to the senator. Glenn then labeled Roberts's testimony "false."

Meanwhile, a federal grand jury was investigating whether the NRC had been lied to about compliance with fire-safety rules by the [D. C. Cook Plant Nuclear Plant] in Michigan. In September 1985, the NRC's solicitor reminded Roberts's legal aide that the prosecutors had asked to attend any meetings between NRC commissioners and Cook officials. But none was invited to Roberts's office for a ninety-minute meeting he and his aide had with a Cook lawyer, according to documents released by the House Interior and Insular Affairs Subcommittee.[2]

■

THE FOXES WHO GUARDED THE CHICKEN COOPS–VIII

MARK S. FOWLER
Chairman, Federal Communications Commission 1981–1987

". . . the Commission should, so far as possible, defer to a broadcaster's judgment about how best to compete for viewers and listeners because this serves the public interest."[1]

■ The quote signaled what Fowler was setting out to, and

[2] Numerous reports by Cass Peterson and others, *Washington Post,* April 22 to June 20, 1987.
[1] Speech, International Radio and Television Society, September 1981.

did, achieve: effective repeal of the requirement in the Federal Communications Act of 1934 that an applicant for a broadcast license demonstrate how issuance of renewal would "serve the public interest, convenience, and necessity."

Fowler was communications counsel to Ronald Reagan in his 1976 and 1980 presidential campaigns, Long before Reagan's reign, to be sure, a license to use the public's airwaves was often called "a license to steal," because of startling profits in using it and in selling the station. But Fowler led the Commission into making it into a license for broadcasters to steal more, More, MORE by killing an antitrafficking rule barring the buyer of a TV station from selling it for at least three years, while wiping out obligations for public service (by, for example, abolishing the Fairness Doctrine, which compelled balanced coverage of controversial issues).

TV critic Tom Shales wrote that Fowler also struck a "deregulatory death blow at the tradition that station owners should be "held accountable at license renewal time. Stations now have no official mandate to air regular, locally responsible, public affairs programs. They are free instead to turn that pesky old public service time into money-making time . . ."[2]

[2] *Washington Post,* June 1, 1987.

THE MOLE

PATRICK S. KORTEN
Director of Public Affairs, then Executive
Assistant Director,
Office of Policy and Communications,
Office of Personnel Management
1981–1985

"It's always nice to be back among fellow right-wing nuts."

■ Korten's tongue wasn't necessarily far back in his cheek when he made this remark at the convention of the Young Americans for Freedom in Boston in August 1981. "Clearly," said the panel moderator who introduced him, "Pat is a right-wing fanatic just like the rest of us, despite his years in the media." The *New York Times*'s Dudley Clendinen also wrote:

" 'In fact,' the moderator gibed, 'you might say he was the conservative's mole in that CBS affiliate in Washington' [he'd been a WTOP radio news announcer].

"Mr Korten smiled at the remark, then explained his new job [at OPM] this way: 'Suffice it to say that it was we who advised Drew Lewis [then Secretary of Transportation]how to go about firing the air traffic controllers.' That drew a cheer from the room."

Clendinen reported that "some 50 graduates or present members of the Young Americans for Freedom have been appointed to the White House staff," while others "are

---

New York Times, August 22, 1981.

sprinkled throughout the Administration, and still others make up much of the conservatives' fund-raising apparatus, which may bring in $50 million this year [1981]."

THE CHOIR LEADER

JAMES V. LACY
Director, Office of Export Trading Company Affairs,
Department of Commerce
1984–1987
General Counsel, Consumer Product Safety Commission,
March 1987–

"Holding copies of 'The YAF Songbook,' the euphoric choir flipped from page to page and roared out the ditties," the New York Times said in a report on the convention of the Young Americans for Freedom in Boston in August 1981. "On the first page are two selections, which, Mr. Lacy said,

" 'We all know by heart.' . . .

"The [second], rendered to the tune of "Deck the Halls with Boughs of Holly,' is this:
"Deck the halls with Commie corpses
"Fa la la la la la la la la
"Tis the time to be remorseless
"Fa la la la la la la la la

"Wield we now our sharp stiletti
"Fa la la la la la la la la
"Carve the pinks into confetti
"Fa la la la la la la la la"

■ President Reagan, himself on the YAF advisory board, sent a filmed message in which he said, "You must continue to provide the kind of philosophical and practical training which offers alternatives to today's youth in order to develop the next generation of leaders for America."

■

THE DEMOCRACY PROJECTOR

CHARLES Z. WICK
Director, United States Information Agency
1981—

". . . co-ordinating the information and sensitivities . . . to implement various communications and approaches to assist the infrastructure of the legal, business and religious communities."

■ This babble was in the first draft of Wick's attempt to explain "Project Democracy," a plan of President Reagan's to nourish the "infrastructure of democracy" in other countries with $85 million. Wick had been chosen to run the project. The draft emerged at a Senate Foreign

---

Washington Post, March 3, 1983.

Relations Committee hearing along with some organization charts which, according to Senator Christopher J. Dodd (D–Conn.), "made Rube Goldberg look like a computer chip."

One was headed "National Security Decision Directive on Public Diplomacy," and to columnist Mary McGrory it appeared especially ominous. "It showed an International Political Committee," she wrote, "which sounded as if its chairman would be Yuri V. Andropov—against whom the whole effort is directed.

" 'In God's name,' said chairman, Charles R. Percy (R–Ill.), 'who is really in charge?'

" 'Frankly,' said Wick, 'there is a lot of confusion in the government . . .' "

THE TAPEWORM

CHARLES Z. WICK
Director, United States Information Agency
1981—

"I've never done it without telling somebody."

■ Columnist William Safire and reporter Jane Perlez reported in December 1983 that Wick had secretly taped his office phone conversations with government officials, his staff, and friends, and that the proof was in transcripts and in statements by his aides. Those secretly taped included: Walter H. Annenberg, former ambassador to Britain, and, like Wick, an intimate friend of Ronald Reagan's; Caspar W. Weinberger, Jr., who is the son of the former secretary of defense, and who worked for Wick at the USIA; Kenneth L. Adelman, director of the Arms

Control and Disarmament Agency; Geoffrey Swaebe, ambassador to Belgium, and Kirk Douglas, the actor.

Wick first claimed he had always informed the other party when a conversation was being recorded. But when several of the conversants said Wick had not told them of this practice, Wick conceded he had not always mentioned that he was recording the conversation. "I often advised the caller that I was recording the conversation or a portion of it, but in haste I did not do this consistently," Wick said in a statement. "I may have been insufficiently sensitive . . ."[1]

Wick told the *Times* he had removed the taping gear from his Dictaphone, "a year ago or more" because "I didn't want it misunderstood" around the agency, adding, "I've never done it without telling somebody . . ."

"Mr. Wick, who angrily refused to continue the interview after 15 minutes, acknowledged that he had been warned 'some time ago' by Jonathan W. Sloat, then the general counsel to the [USIA], that he should not tape without permission."[1]

Later, Wick said, "I meant no offense to anyone and apologize if any was taken."[2] Had he ever taped Senator Mark O. Hatfield (R–Ore.)? Wick was asked. "Absolutely not." Had he taped Annenberg? "No." These answers were "untrue," Safire said.[2] Despite all this, Reagan praised the "splendid job" Wick had done, adding, "I don't think that [he] is a dishonorable man in any way."[3]

[1] *New York Times,* December 28, 1983.
[2] *New York Times* (news story and column), December 29, 1983.
[3] *Washington Post,* January 7, 1984.

THE FOLKS WHO DON'T HAVE A BIGOTED BONE IN THEIR BODIES–I

MARIANNE MELE HALL
Chairman, Copyright Royalty Tribunal
1985

Blacks in America

". . . insist on preserving their jungle freedoms, their women, their avoidance of personal responsibility and their abhorrence of the work ethic, [and] have inherited a different set of aptitudes, values, mores, goals and life styles over a period of 10,000 years."

■ These were among the bigotries in a chapter of *Foundations of Sand: A Hard Look at the Soft Sciences*. The co-authors of the 1982 book were: Lawrence Hafstad, a retired General Motors vice president; John Morse, a retired Navy captain affiliated with High Frontier, Inc., and, lastly, Ms. Hall, an editor of the 1981 High Frontier paper in which the "Star Wars" missile-defense plan was first proposed.

The acknowledgments in *Foundations* . . . convey Morse's thanks to Hafstad for his "brilliant ideas . . . and [to Hall] for expressing them so effectively." She was "the professional writer/editor," Hafstad told a reporter.

President Reagan chose Hall in 1985 to head the Royalty Tribunal, which sets the fees cable-television operators

---

Keith B. Richburg, *Washington Post,* May 1, 2, 3, 7, 8, 9, and 13, 1985, and May 18, 1987.

pay to use copyrighted materials, and collects and apportions them among copyright owners. She listed herself in a Senate confirmation questionnaire as "coauthor" of *Foundations*.

Shortly thereafter, *Broadcasting* magazine excerpted the chapter, setting off a Mele melee in which she came under fire for helping to write a book disfigured by racism. After refusing to say whether she agreed with the insults, she tried to disassociate herself, calling them "repugnant." But, under White House pressure, she resigned on May 8, later becoming counsel of the right-wing Washington Legal Foundation.

■

THE FOLKS WHO DON'T HAVE A BIGOTED BONE IN THEIR BODIES–II

CHARLES Z. WICK
Director, United States Information Agency
1981—

". . . some of them have marvelous minds, those black people over there."[1]

■ Inspired by a visit to Africa, Wick's discovery was a transcontinental echo of the insight volunteered by his good friend Ronald Reagan after a visit to Latin America. Had the trip changed the President's views of the region? a reporter asked. "You'd be surprised," he said. "They're all individual countries."[2]

---

[1] Mary McGrory, *Washington Post,* March 3, 1983.
[2] *Washington Post,* December 6, 1982.

The occasion for Wick's comment was a Senate Foreign Relations Committee hearing on "Project Democracy." Reagan had proposed this costly, fuzzy scheme for promoting the "infrastructure of democracy" around the globe, and had put Wick in charge.

Senator Nancy Landon Kassebaum (R–Kan.) said that a trip to Africa had persuaded her that people there need health care and basic education more than Project Democracy English lessons. Noting that he too had visited Africa, Wick remarked without guile, ". . . some of them have marvelous minds . . ."[1]

"Margaret Thatcher's a great prime minister. She's also a woman."

■ Moments later:

"She's a great lady. When I say she's a woman, I'm talking about people who are superior to men. Please don't print what I just said; I'll never get back to London.[2]

■ Thatcher's opposition to the invasion of Grenada was the genesis of Wick's gender-based generic progression: condescension to genuflection to sniveling. The trigger was a question put to him after he gave a talk to California newspaper publishers in San Francisco.[3]

■

---

[3] Associated Press, December 3, 1983.

THE FOLKS WHO DON'T HAVE A BIGOTED BONE IN THEIR BODIES–III

JEFFERSON B. SESSIONS III
Nominee, U.S. District Judge, Southern District of Alabama
1986

Until he learned that some Ku Klux Klan members "smoked pot,"

"I used to think they're okay."

■ This was one of the remarks attributed to Sessions in sworn statements by four Justice Department civil rights lawyers who had worked with him. Their depositions were taken by Senate Judiciary Committee staff members on the eve of the confirmation hearing that doomed his nomination.

In 1985, Sessions, the U.S. attorney in Mobile, had unsuccessfully prosecuted Albert Turner, a former aide to the Reverend Dr. Martin Luther King, Jr., for alleged voting fraud. Turner was one of several black civil rights leaders in Alabama who were targeted in a series of such failed prosecutions. The record that made Sessions deserve elevation to the federal bench, in the eyes of Ronald Reagan, made him anathema to advocates of civil rights.

At the committee hearing, Sessions commented on other remarks the lawyers swore he'd made.

No, he didn't remember calling the National Association for the Advancement of Colored People "a pinko or-

Howard Kurtz, *Washington Post,* and Lena Williams, *New York Times,* March 14, 1986.

ganization" that "hates white people," but, yes, being "loose with my tongue on occasion," he "may have said something about the NAACP being un-American or Communist, but I meant no harm . . ."

No, he hadn't called a black official in Mobile a "nigger," but, yes, he'd agreed with another person who called a prominent white civil rights attorney "a disgrace to his race." He added: "I don't know why I would have said that . . . I certainly don't believe that."

Yes, he'd said that the NAACP and the National Council of Churches are "considered un-American . . . when they involve themselves in promoting un-American positions" on foreign policy. Such as? He was able to cite only support of "the Sanctuary movement [for refugees] and the Sandinistas."

The committee rejected the nomination. Senator Howell Heflin (D–Ala.) cast the deciding vote, and, on June 6, was accused of "treason" by Sessions's hometown paper, the *Mobile Register*. On July 9, Sessions withdrew his name from nomination.

THE FOLKS WHO DON'T HAVE A BIGOTED BONE IN THEIR BODIES–IV

J. PETER GRACE
Chairman, President's Private Sector Survey on Cost Control in the Federal Government 1982–1984

"Nine hundred thousand [Puerto Ricans] live in New York, and they're all on food stamps, so this food stamp program is basically a Puerto

Rican program. I've got nothing against Puerto Ricans, but this is a little much."

■ In the last fiscal year of the Carter administration, the budget for food stamps was $12.7 billion, including $1.04 billion for Puerto Rico. The first fiscal year of the Reagan administration brought reductions of about 10 percent—to $11.5 billion, including $904 million for Puerto Rico. After citing these figures, in a prepared speech to the American Feed and Grain Manufacturers' Association in Dallas, Grace departed from his text to attack the food-stamp outlays for Puerto Ricans in New York, who constitute about 45 percent of the total living in the U.S. mainland.

Representative Robert Garcia (D–N.Y.), leader of the Congressional Hispanic Caucus, asked President Reagan to request Grace to resign, calling his textual deviation "as racist as anything I have ever heard in my 17 years of elective office." The Commonwealth's representative in the House, Resident Commissioner Baltasar Corrado, also pressed for Grace's resignation, calling his comments an "affront and insult to Puerto Ricans . . . on the island as well as on the mainland."

A White House spokesman responded: "Mr. Grace was giving his personal views and we have no comment on [them]."

■

Bruce Bakke, United Press International, May 28, 1982

THE FOLKS WHO DON'T HAVE A BIGOTED BONE IN THEIR BODIES–V

JAMES G. WATT
Secretary of the Interior
1981–1983

Watt named the five members of the Federal Commission on Fair Market Value Policy for Federal Coal Leasing, created by Congress to investigate charges that Watt's program for leasing coal wasted $100 million of the taxpayers' money. Not only did he pick three Democrats, but he described the commission as having

". . . every kind of mixture you can have. I have a black. I have a woman, two Jews and a cripple. And we have talent" [1]

■ One commissioner said, "I am the Jew and the cripple, if you want to call someone who has a paralyzed right arm a cripple." Another said Watt had phoned him to say he had intended to make a joke.[1]

"I never use the words Democrats and Republicans. It's liberals and Americans."[2]

---

[1] Martin Crutsinger in an Associated Press report on September 21, 1983, on Watt's appearance that day before an audience of business lobbyists at the Chamber of Commerce of the United States.
[2] Watt said this to farmers in the San Joaquin Valley in California at a luncheon that was closed to the press. But one of the farmers made a tape and gave it to the *Fresno Bee* for a page-one story (cited in the

". . . I didn't understand the environmentalists. I thought they were concerned about the resources and the environment. They are not. They are political activists, a left-wing cult which seeks to bring down the type of government I believe in."[3]

■

THE FOLKS WHO DON'T HAVE A BIGOTED BONE IN THEIR BODIES–VI

JOHN B. CROWELL, JR.
Assistant Secretary for Natural Resources and Environment,
Department of Agriculture
1981–1984

On the one hand, most members of the Sierra Club and the National Audubon Society have

". . . a genuine concern about the treatment of our natural resources. On the other hand, I'm

---

Washington Post, November 30, 1981). Later, Watt said it was a "joke" *(U.S. News & World Report,* June 14, 1982).

[3] Interview, *Forest Industry Affairs Letter,* February 1982; excerpted by United Press International, March 23, 1982.

sure the organizations are also infiltrated by people who have very strong ideas about socialism and even communism."[1]

Crowell apologized the next day:

"I want to make it perfectly clear that I have no reason to think that the Audubon Society, the Sierra Club or any other conservation organization [is] in any way un-American. In fact, I believe to the contrary, and I very much regret the confusion and the wrong implication that [have] come from it."[2]

■ The Audubon Society, the Sierra Club, and the Wilderness Society had been among the sternest critics of Crowell's policy of increasing the timber cut in national forests. Crowell apparently felt a pull but also a tug: while he'd been a long-time member of the Audubon and Wilderness societies, he'd also been general counsel for Louisiana-Pacific, a major timber company. In apologizing, he said he'd erred in saying that the environmentalist organizations could be infiltrated, and that on seeing his comments in a newspaper, he was "mortified and shocked."[2]

■

[1] *Albuquerque Journal,* March 12, 1982.
[2] Ward Sinclair, *Washington Post,* March 24, 1982, and Sonja Hillgren, United Press International, March 25, 1982.

THE SWEET YOUNG THING

DEBORAH GORE DEAN

*Nominee, Assistant Secretary for Community
Planning and Development, Department of
Housing and Urban Development
1987*

"Why are they so concerned about a little job
here at HUD and some little girl trying to get a
job?"

The little job controls about $3.7 billion in federal funds—
more than 40 percent of HUD's budget—and a $77,500
salary. The little girl—a 1980 graduate of Georgetown
University in Washington—said in her employment record
that for nine years starting in 1972, she held jobs as a
restaurant hostess, manager, and disc jockey; as a part-
time bartender; and in publishing and public relations.

In mid-1981, six months after Ronald Reagan took office, Dean became a special assistant at the Department of
Energy. In November 1982 she went to HUD as director
of the Executive Secretariat and special assistant to Secretary Samuel R. Pierce, Jr. In June 1984 she became his
executive assistant.

In 1987, when she was thirty-three, the President nominated her as an assistant secretary, and housing groups
complained. "I do not have the high degree of qualifications that some people who have had this job have had,"
she conceded to a reporter. But, she said, she'd worked
hard, and Pierce "thinks I'm an outstanding nominee and

Michael Isikoff, *Washington Post,* September 22, 1987.

Ronald Reagan agrees with him." Nevertheless, the Senate returned the nomination to the President in August 1987.

Dean is the stepdaughter of John N. Mitchell, who was President Nixon's attorney general.

■

THE HUMANIST

PATRICK J. BUCHANAN
Assistant to President Reagan and Director of
White House Communications
1985–1987

"The poor homosexuals. They have declared war on nature, and now nature is exacting an awful retribution."[1]

■ The "awful retribution" is, of course, AIDS, a disease attacking the immune system which almost invariably is fatal. AIDS is transmitted through the blood and, possibly, other bodily fluids. While the first cases of AIDS to be diagnosed in the United States occurred among homosexual males, within a short time AIDS began to appear among other groups: drug addicts who shared needles; persons who had been infected by transfusions of contaminated blood; and heterosexuals contracting the disease from a bisexual partner.

Buchanan frequently writes widely published columns expounding some of the less charitable views of "conservative" Republicans. Some of his comments begin in

[1] Column of June 23, 1983, cited in the *Washington Post*, February 4, 1987.

sympathy and end with a twist of the knife. Others simply omit information, as in the following quotation:

"That blacks under apartheid are second-class citizens is undeniable. But apartheid is not the worst situation facing Africans today. Not remotely. If it were, they wouldn't be pouring into South Africa from such 'liberated' zones as Mozambique."[2]

Buchanan fails to relate that the reason blacks seek refuge in South Africa is that for seven years Mozambique has been terrorized by Renamo, an organization fighting against the Mozambique government. At least 100,000 people have been killed and another 100,000 have starved to death. Ironically, the sponsor of Renamo is the South African government. South Africa pursues a cynical policy of supporting groups like Renamo and using other means to foster strife and economic upheaval in neighboring black-ruled countries to deter them from aiding South Africa's black majority in its fight against apartheid.[3]

[2] Column of January 16, 1985, cited in the *Washington Post,* February 4, 1987.
[3] *The New Yorker,* November 16, 1987.

THE WITNESS AGAINST HIMSELF

EDWIN MEESE III
Attorney General
1985—

"The *Miranda* decision was wrong. We managed very well in this country for 175 years without it. It only helps guilty defendants."[1]

■ The Supreme Court's *Miranda* ruling of 1966 requires police officers, before questioning a suspect in a criminal case, to advise him as follows: he has "the right to remain silent"; "anything said can and will be used against the individual in court"; he has the "right to have counsel present at the interrogation," and, if he is an "indigent," he may have "a lawyer . . . appointed to represent him."

Before *Miranda,* according to studies cited by the Court, police commonly tried to compel confessions by interrogating suspects endlessly, not informing them of their undisputed right to silence, or beating them. The bar to a compulsion to speak accords with the letter and spirit of the Fifth Amendment, ratified in 1791: "No person . . . shall be compelled in any criminal case to be a witness against himself . . ."

Meese's position offends leaders of respected police organizations and legal historians and scholars. *"Miranda* isn't the problem with crime," says Gerald Arenberg, executive director of the National Association of Police Chiefs. "We have never noticed that *Miranda* itself has been a problem with police investigations." Without *Miranda,* says Minneapolis Police Chief Anthony Bouza,

---

[1] *U.S. News & World Report,* October 14, 1985.

"you're sure to return to the days of the third degree and the cops beating shit out of people."[2]

The top law-enforcement officer "knows nothing about the history of criminal justice in this country if he thinks that for 175 years before *Miranda* we managed very well," said Leonard Levy of California's Claremont Graduate School of Law. "In fact, we managed disgracefully."[3] *Miranda* "has made clear that everyone's got some rights, even the most despicable subject," said Yale Kamisar of the University of Michigan Law School.[3]

■

THE PRESUMED INNOCENT

EDWIN MEESE III
Counselor to the President
1981–1985
Attorney General
1985—

"If a person is innocent of a crime, then he is not a suspect."[1]

■ Thus did the attorney general, in a taped interview, repudiate the presumption of innocence owed to *every* suspect. Although he'd reviewed the transcript before publication, he misspoke—so said his spokesman in the ensuing up-

[2] Jeffrey Toobin, *New Republic*, February 16, 1987.
[3] Stephen Wermiel, *Wall Street Journal*, September 8, 1987.
[1] *U.S. News & World Report*, October 14, 1985.

roar.[2] But Meese himself, months later, claimed he'd been misquoted.[3] This helps to explain why the highest law-enforcement officer in the land isn't always accorded the presumption of being a reliable truthteller, particularly when he tries to take his old friend Ronald Reagan off the hook.

Consider the issue of tax breaks for segregated schools. The policy had been to deny exemptions, but in 1982, the White House decided to grant them, setting off a flap. Counselor Meese claimed the President hadn't known of the new policy. Rather, he said, he had revoked existing policy on his own, in a court case involving Bob Jones University.

Only three days later, Reagan drove a spear into Meese's credibility, saying, "I'm the originator of the whole thing." Two days after that the spear was twisted in the wound by the leak of a memo a White House aide had written to Reagan weeks before the policy shift was announced. The memo disclosed that a Republican congressman had urged Reagan to intervene in the Bob Jones case. The President scribbled in the margin of the memo, "I think we should."[2]

Such episodes were prologue to the falsities spoken by Meese on November 25, 1986, such as: Reagan was unaware of the shipment of U.S. arms to Iran; no one in the government authorized the first arms shipment; and Israel was responsible for the sales and diversion.[3]

---

[2] The *Washington Post*'s Howard Kurtz, in a *Post* article on July 19, 1987, based on his three years' coverage of Meese.
[3] *Newsweek,* July 13, 1987.

THE JUDICIAL SCHOLAR

DANIEL A. MANION

Judge, Seventh U.S. Circuit Court of Appeals
1986—

Demonstrators against the war in Vietnam

". . . should be penned up . . . Why are all these people, some [of whom] are even convicted criminals, going around the country and . . . advocating communism, why are they allowed to run free?"[1]

■ By December 1987, Ronald Reagan had named 332 of the 743 U.S. District, Appeals, and Supreme courts judges. Manion, the 268th, was a front-runner in the race for the title of "Least Distinguished." When the Senate Judiciary Committee asked him to list the ten "most significant" cases of his thirteen-year legal career in South Bend, Indiana, he cited one in which a car dealer was accused of misrepairing a Volkswagen Rabbit.[2]

In the 1970s, he and his late father, Clarence, a John Birch Society leader, hosted *The Manion Forum* on hundreds of radio and television stations. It was on the *Forum* in 1971 that Daniel aired his dedication to the constitutional rights of Vietnam War protesters, as embodied in the introductory quote.

During another *Forum* broadcast, in 1971, father asked son what "things . . . make you suspicious of the supremacy of the Supreme Court?"

---

[1] Howard Kurtz, *Washington Post,* May 1 and May 6, 1986.
[2] Paul Houston, *Los Angeles Times,* July 13, 1986.

"It seems to have gone into regulating schools . . . tries to redistrict the legislature . . . took prayer out of public schools . . . And now it seems they've allowed pornography both on the newsstands and in the movie theaters."[1]

A book by the late Representative Larry P. McDonald (R–Ga.) said that the Court's 1954 school desegregation decision was unconstitutional. On the *Forum* in 1977, Manion called the book "one of the finest summaries of the history of our country." In 1986, however, he told the committee he wasn't sure he'd read it.

As an Indiana state senator in 1981, Manion sponsored a bill to allow posting of the Ten Commandments in public schools. Two months earlier, the Supreme Court had barred such postings.[1]

■

THE SWITCH HITTER

CIRCUIT JUDGE ROBERT H. BORK
*Nominee, Supreme Court of the United States
1987*

"The framers seem to have had no coherent theory of free speech . . . The First Amendment, like the rest of the Bill of Rights, appears to have been a hastily drafted document upon which little thought was expended."[1]

---

[1] *Indiana Law Journal,* Fall 1971.

"Constitutional protection should be afforded only to speech that is explicitly political."

Judge Bork wrote the above in 1971, while a Yale law professor, but in 1987, hoping to become an associate justice of the Supreme Court, he testified to striking conversions:

". . . I have the greatest respect for the Bill of Rights, . . ."[2]

"I simply do not have a narrow view of the First Amendment's protection of freedom of speech and press."

Saying that First Amendment protections were limited to explicitly political speech was:

". . . a dumb idea."[2]

The Supreme Court held in 1969 that the First Amendment protected advocacy of law-breaking so long as it posed no danger of "imminent lawless action." The ruling was:

---

[2] Senate Judiciary Committee hearing, September 15 and 16, 1987.

"... fundamentally wrong,"[1] "It's right."[2]
"... I have no desire to overturn it."[3]

THE UTILITY OUTFIELDER
CIRCUIT JUDGE ROBERT H. BORK

"The cases are identical."

■ To Bork, lust can be sexual, or it can be economic—
they're both the same thing. He made his point with two
cases. *Griswold* v. *Connecticut* involved the privacy of sexual relations between a man and a woman and their right
to decide whether to have a child. In 1965, the Supreme
Court struck down a law making use of contraceptives a
crime. The second case, hypothesized by Bork, involved
profitability. A power company and a customer join in
suing to have a smoke-pollution law held unconstitutional.

"The cases are identical.

"In *Griswold,* a husband and wife assert that they
wish to have sexual relations without fear of unwanted
children. The law impairs their sexual gratifications [a
word Bork prefers to "rights"]. The State can assert,
... that the majority [of the electorate] finds the use
of contraceptives immoral. Knowledge that it takes

[3] Hearing, September 17, 1987.
Indiana Law Journal, Fall 1971.

place and that the State makes no effort to inhibit it causes the majority anguish, impairs their gratifications.

"The electrical company asserts that it wishes to produce electricity at low cost in order to reach a wide market and make profits. Its customer asserts that he wants a lower cost so that prices can be held low. The smoke pollution regulation impairs his and the company's stockholders' economic gratifications. The State can assert not only that the majority prefers clean air to lower prices, but also that the absence of the regulation impairs the majority's physical and aesthetic gratifications . . . The only course for a principled Court is to let the majority have its way in both cases . . .

"There is no principled way to decide . . . that one form of gratification is more worthy than another. Why is sexual gratification more worthy than moral gratification? Why is sexual gratification nobler than economic gratification?"

THE COLOR-BLIND ENFORCER

WILLIAM BRADFORD REYNOLDS
Assistant Attorney General for Civil Rights
1981—

"It must be remembered that we are all—each of us—a minority in this country, a minority of one."

■

THE GENERALISSIMO

ALEXANDER M. HAIG, JR.
SECRETARY OF STATE
1981–1982

"There are 40 people here. I don't know who they are!"

■ In the early days of the Reagan administration, David ^ Stockman, director of the Office of Management and get, was trying to slash spending government-wide, ε Haig was trying to protect the budgets of the State Department and the Agency for International Development from Stockman's ax. After preliminary skirmishing, they arranged a "low key" meeting in what was called the

---

Interview with Juan Williams, *Washington Post Magazine,* January 10, 1988.

"Cutting Room." Stockman recalled how Haig left him on the Cutting Room floor:

" 'Low key' it wasn't. Normally, ten to fifteen people attended Cutting Room sessions. When we walked into it this time, it was packed to the rafters with Haig's entourage of forty to fifty people from State and [AID]. Immediately Haig began to complain. To quote his words: 'I can't make decisions in a roomful of people. There are forty people here. I don't know who they are!'

"It was . . . surreal. They were *his* people—he had brought them. And now he was saying he couldn't be expected to decide anything in their presence. Not surprisingly, the meeting broke up without having produced any results."

■

THE VICTORS–I

VICTOR A. SCHROEDER
President, U.S. Synthetic Fuels Corporation
1981–1983

"Where else are you going to find people to do work the way you need it done, other than people that you know or that someone knows?"[1]

■ Schroeder, an Atlanta shopping-center developer, and his long-time business partner, Edward E. Noble, an Oklahoma oil and gas multimillionaire, led President-elect Reagan's Synfuels's transition team. Then Reagan named Noble chairman of the quasi-independent agency, which

---

[1] *Business Week,* June 28, 1982.

had $14.7 billion available to finance development projects for alternative energy sources. Noble named Schroeder president, at $69,500 a year (increased to $135,000 in May 1982 after he hinted at quitting). Schroeder's wife, Kathryne, became Noble's secretary at $32,000.[1]

In March 1983, on the eve of a board vote on Schroeder's plan to reorganize the agency, he had a late-night conversation in a hotel room with Milton M. Masson, Jr., a fellow director. As a result, Masson agreed to support the plan; Schroeder agreed to lobby a friend at Mobil Corporation's land-development subsidiary to retain Masson's engineering-design firm.

Two months later, three of the seven agency directors urged Schroeder's dismissal for improprieties and mismanagement. In July, at a hearing of a Senate Governmental Affairs subcommittee, he insisted that he and Masson hadn't scratched each other's backs at the late-night meeting. But Donald Thibeau, Noble's executive assistant, had witnessed the conversation, was subpoenaed, and testified that Schroeder and Masson "came to an understanding."

Schroeder admitted he had awarded consulting contracts to fifty-one persons without competitive bidding. "It makes no sense to put up personal services for competitive bid," he said. "Where else are you going to find people to do work . . . ?"

He could have bought his home in a Washington suburb for $305,500, but he paid an extra $19,500 in commission and charged it to the agency as a cost of relocating, although he'd never sold his home in Atlanta. Agency auditors disallowed the $19,500, and he repaid it. He resigned as president on August 18 1983,[2] but remained a director until the demise of the Corporation in April 1986.

---

[2] Howard Kurtz, *Washington Post,* August 9 and 19, 1983.

THE VICTORS–II

VICTOR M. THOMPSON, JR.
President, U.S. Synthetic Fuels Corporation
1981–1984

"It is a tragedy when dedicated citizens . . . can't serve without coming under political siege."

■ Thompson was chairman and chief executive of Utica Bankshares Company, a Tulsa, Oklahoma, firm that suffered large losses. Seeking an infusion of capital, Thompson tried to sell Utica stock to a San Antonio company. While wooing its owner, Thompson voted four times to grant Synfuels subsidies to two of the company's subsidiaries.

In mid-1983, the Securities and Exchange Commission began a probe into whether Utica had violated securities laws by overstating profits and not reporting problem loans that ultimately caused the bank to lose more than $20 million. Thompson didn't tell his fellow Synfuels directors either about the negotiations—ultimately unsuccessful—in which he tried to sell Utica stock, or about the SEC investigation.

Kept in the dark, the board elected Thompson president at a salary of $135,000, making him the highest-paid federal official after President Reagan.

Two weeks later, in February 1984, the SEC filed a civil complaint against Utica. In April, Owen J. Malone, Synfuels's ethics officer, told the directors that because the SEC probe was clearly material to Thompson's fitness for

---

Michael Isikoff, *Washington Post,* April 27 and 28, 1984.

the presidency, his failure to disclose it to the board violated its ethics policy. A few days later, the board and Malone learned of the negotiations to sell Utica stock. On April 26, 1984, Thompson resigned as president, but vowed to remain on the board; hours later, he resigned as a director too, giving up a $10,000 director's stipend.

"It is a tragedy when dedicated citizens . . . can't serve without coming under political siege," he said in his resignation letter.

███

THE ELECTION BUYER

LEE ATWATER
Assistant to the President for Political and Governmental Affairs 1981–1983

Elizabeth Drew of *The New Yorker:* "I asked Atwater what he thought the impact of all the money the Republicans could put into an election would be. He replied,

"I think the story of this off-year election is that we've marshalled our resources and bought one or two Senate seats and 15 to 20 House seats, and that's really good."

Drew interviewed Atwater in the fall of 1982, and the quoted material appeared first in *The New Yorker* on December 6, 1982, and then in her book, *Politics and Money: The New Road to Corruption* (New York: Macmillan) in 1983.

Drew continued: "As things turned out, the Republicans lost 26 House seats. Republican Party officials themselves said that if it hadn't been for the money the losses would have been greater. The two parties broke even in the Senate, but a switch of about 70,000 votes in five states would have given those seats to the Democrats. In all of those states but one (Nevada, where a Democratic incumbent senator lost), the winner outspent the loser. In fact, the winners outspent the losers in 27 of the 33 Senate races. In five of the six races where the margin of victory was four percent or less, the winners spent twice as much as the losers."

THE PROPHETS–I

CHRISTOPHER C. SUNDSETH
Treasury Department Economist
1984–1985

'When you die, you will give your account to Jesus Christ, your Creator, who happens to be Christian. I hope you are prepared."

The warning grew out of a speech in which the Reverend Robert J. Billings, an official in the Department of Education's Denver office, referred to the United States as a "Christian nation." A staff member, Thomas Tancredo, distributed the speech at taxpayers' expense.

In a postcard to Tancredo, Gerald B. Lieb, a California lawyer, protested distribution of the speech by the govern-

New York Times, August 8, August 13, and November 13, 1985.

ment, pointing out that under the Constitution the United States has never been a Christian nation.

In Washington, where Treasury had assigned him to the Inter-American Development Bank, Sundseth heard about Lieb's postcard from an unidentified person and decided to write to the lawyer on his personal stationery.

"This country was founded by Christians who were escaping the same kind of small-minded tripe you espouse," Sundseth told Lieb in a postscript to his letter.

In November 1985, Treasury dismissed Sundseth, but attributed the dismissal "entirely to staff cutbacks."

■

THE PROPHETS–II

JAMES G. WATT
Secretary of the Interior
1981–1983

"I do not know how many future generations we can count on before the Lord returns."[1]

■ This was Watt's response to a philosophical question about his views on the preservation of natural resources for future generations.

"Compromise is not in my vocabulary. I don't know what compromise is, and I'm not going to learn. Some people in this town can't deal with

---

[1] Bill Prochnau, *Washington Post,* June 30, 1981.

hat. As a consequence, my usefulness will xpire."[2]

Eighteen days before resigning, Watt, speaking of his wn future, said he not only expected to serve throughout second Reagan administration, i.e., from January 1985 January 1989, but had

". . . started negotiating to serve the full ight years with George Bush."[3]

THE PROPHETS–III

DAVID A. STOCKMAN
Director, Office of Management and Budget 1981–1985

"Evidence that the federal government has gone off the deep end in the conduct of its fiscal affairs continues to mount: $950 billion in red nk has accumulated from Reagan's first five budgets, along with a virtual guarantee that the emaining three Reagan budgets will add $550 billion more to the total (based on momentum

---

Interview in the *Forest Industry Affairs Letter,* February 1982; cited by United Press International, March 23, 1982.
Reply to a reporter's question after a talk at the Chamber of Commerce f the United States, September 21, 1983.

from the record 1986 deficit). Thus, in eight years of direction by the most conservative administration in modern times, the federal government's spending will have exceeded its income by the staggering sum of *$1.5 trillion.* The next President will inherit a publicly held federal debt nearly *triple* that accumulated by all of Ronald Reagan's thirty-nine predecessors."

Introductory paragraph to the chapter ("Postscript") that Stockman wrote especially for the Avon Books (1987) edition of *The Triumph of Politics.*

"As disappointed as I may be in some who served me, I'm still the one who must answer to the American people for this behavior."

—President Ronald Wilson Reagan,
Address to the Nation,
March 4, 1987

PART TWO

WHY NOT THE WORST?

PRESIDENT RON'S PURSUIT OF EXCELLENCE–I

[A reporter] Question: "Mr. President, more than a dozen members of your administration have left under some sort of a cloud, and this is what the Democrats are calling the sleaze factor. Are you concerned that voters might think there's a lack of integrity in the people that you've hired . . . ?"

"Well, in the first place, I reject the use of the word 'sleaze,' and I'll repeat what I have said many times before, and over a period of years.

"I believe the halls of government are as sacred as our temples of worship, and nothing but the highest integrity is required of those who serve in the government . . .

"Now, I will be the first to remove anyone in the administration that does not have the highest integrity."

—News conference, April 4, 1984

I
IN AND OUT OF COURT

Indicted

LYN NOFZIGER, former Assistant to the President for Political Affairs: On trial early in 1988 on four counts of violating ethics laws in lobbying former Reagan administration colleagues on behalf of two defense contractors, including the scandal-plagued Wedtech Corporation (see A Meese unto Himself, page 102) and a labor union within a year of leaving the White House in 1982. He has pleaded not guilty. A federal judge in October 1987 refused to dismiss the indictment.

On February 11, as this book went to press, Nofziger was found guilty of illegal lobbying.

Convicted

MICHAEL K. DEAVER, former White House Deputy Chief of Staff: Convicted in 1987 of lying to a congressional subcommittee and a federal grand jury about his lobbying activities after leaving the White House in 1985. He was found guilty on three of five perjury counts and faced a possible sentence of fifteen years in prison and a $22,000 fine. During the trial, a former Trans World Airlines executive said Deaver was employed by the company to make contact with Elizabeth Hanford Dole, then transportation secretary. The executive testified that Deaver was paid a $250,000-a-year retainer and was asked to do little but make a telephone call to Dole in 1985. Deaver was found guilty of lying to a House subcommittee about his efforts to obtain a meeting with the President for a trade representative of South Korea, which paid his concern $475,000 a year; of falsely telling a federal grand jury that he had forgotten contacts he made for TWA; and of telling the grand jury he couldn't remember his efforts to help retain a tax policy favorable to domestic manufacturers with factories in Puerto Rico. After the verdict was announced, Deaver said, "I know in my heart that I am innocent," and his attorney said the conviction would be appealed. He is the highest ranking current or former Reagan official to be convicted of a crime.

C. McCLAIN HADDOW, former Chief of Staff, Department of Health and Human Services: Sentenced in 1987 to a year in prison and a $15,000 fine for improperly receiving $55,300 from the government and the nonprofit T. Bear Foundation. A federal judge subsequently refused to throw out the sentence. Haddow was not expected to serve more than ninety days.

ROBERT HILL, former Seattle Regional Chief, Economic Development Administration: Sentenced to six months in prison in 1985 after his conviction for accepting $1,000 from the head of an antipoverty group funded by his agency.

RITA M. LAVELLE, former Assistant Administrator, Environmental Protection Agency: Convicted in 1984 of lying to Congress about the date on which she learned her former employer, Aerojet-General Corporation, had dumped wastes at a California site being investigated by the EPA. She also was convicted of obstructing a congressional inquiry and served part of a six-month prison sentence.

J. WILLIAM PETRO, former U.S. Attorney in Cleveland: Convicted in 1985 of criminal contempt for violating grand jury secrecy and fined $7,500. Petro, who was fired by Reagan in 1984 after the allegations were made, was charged with telling a friend that the man's associates had been named in a sealed indictment for selling counterfeit merchandise.

PAUL THAYER, former Deputy Secretary of Defense: Pleaded guilty in 1985 to obstructing justice and giving false testimony in an insider stock-trading scheme in which he leaked confidential information about companies of which he was a director to his girlfriend, his Dallas stockbroker, and others. The scheme netted eight of his friends more than $1.5 million in illegal profits. He served nineteen months of a four-year prison term. Upon release he reentered the business world by gaining board seats at two small public companies.

PETER E. VOSS, former Vice Chairman, U.S. Postal Service Board of Governors: Pleaded guilty in 1986 to charges of expense fraud and accepting kickbacks; he was sentenced to four years in prison and fined $11,000. Earlier that year, White House officials had recommended Voss—who cochaired Reagan's 1980 Ohio campaign—for the ambassadorship to the Netherlands. (See page 13, The Screener.)

Acquitted

RAYMOND J. DONOVAN, former Secretary of Labor: Acquitted in 1987, along with reputed Bronx mobster William P. Masselli and six others of fraud charges that had forced his resignation in 1985. Donovan, his construction company, and other defendants were accused of defrauding the New York City Transit Authority of $7.4 million in building a still unfinished subway tunnel. The indictment charged them with using as a front a phony minority business company run by a reputed Mafia soldier. An independent counsel secretly examining new allegations that Donovan had lied about seeking $250,000 in kickbacks while in private business decided later in 1987 that there was "insufficient corroborative evidence to support a successful prosecution." Donovan, in a statement, said the charges were "yet another baseless complaint against me. . . .This chapter in my life is now, definitely closed."

THOMAS C. REED, former Special Assistant to the President: Acquitted in 1985 of insider stock-trading charges. Reed, a former Air Force secretary, in 1981 turned a $3,125 investment in his father's company into a $427,000 to $431,000 profit in forty-eight hours. He gave up the profit but denied he had used inside information from his father, a company director, about a merger offer that boosted the value of the firm's stock.

He resigned in 1983 and now is chairman of a prosperous real estate firm near San Francisco.

GEORGE A. SAWYER, former Assistant Secretary of the Navy: Acquitted in 1985 of charges of violating conflict-of-interest laws and lying about the circumstances under which he negotiated a job as a General Dynamics Corporation vice president. He had been accused of concealing that he flew to job interviews at General Dynamics at the company's expense while he still was supervising its Navy shipbuilding contracts.

II
THE NEVER-ENDING DRAMA
OF IRAN-CONTRAGATE

Iran-Contragate is the scandal of an administration that publicly vowed to deal with no terrorists but secretly sold arms to one terrorist nation, Iran, and used some of the proceeds to provide military funding to the Nicaraguan contras—funding that Congress had specifically limited. In November 1987, a House-Senate majority report on a lengthy investigation into the affair charged the Reagan administration with "disdain for the law" and assigned the "ultimate responsibility" for the affair to the President. Reagan appointees implicated in the dealings include:

ELLIOTT ABRAMS, Assistant Secretary of State: Testified in 1986 before the Senate Intelligence Committee that the U.S. had not received money from a foreign government for the contra cause. But a year before, he had gone to London to solicit $10 million from Brunei for the contras. In 1987, he admitted he had been evasive in the earlier hearings; 129 congressmen demanded that he resign, but Secretary of State George P. Shultz, supported Abrams with praise. See page 39, The Loyalists–I.)

GEORGE H. BUSH, Vice President: According to a secret memorandum pieced together by congressional investigators, Bush solidly supported the sale of U.S. weapons to Iran in hopes of freeing American hostages. Bush dismissed the memo as unimportant. Also mentioned as "fully on board this risky operation" in the memo from National Security Adviser *John M. Poindexter* to his predecessor, *Robert C. McFarlane,* were: *William J. Casey, Edwin Meese III, Donald Regan,* Poindexter, and "most importantly, president and VP are solid in taking the position that we have to try." (See pages 25–27, The Inside Dope(ster) I–III.)

WILLIAM J. CASEY, Director, Central Intelligence Agency: Casey, who died in office in 1987, was suspected of lying to Congress about the CIA's involvement in the Iran-Contragate affair. Investigative reporter Bob Woodward, in his book *VEIL: The Secret Wars of the CIA 1981–1987,* said Casey on his deathbed acknowledged knowing about the diversion of profits from Iran arms sales to the contras. Woodward claimed Casey's involvement was much deeper—that the CIA chief "almost drew up the plan" for a secret supply operation to the contras in 1984.

(Among his other alleged exploits were his arranging for the Saudi Arabian intelligence service to attempt an assassination that went wrong and killed eighty innocent people in a Beirut suburb in 1985. In 1982, he traded oil and computer stocks worth $3 million despite his access to sensitive financial intelligence and he refused until 1983 to place his holdings in a blind trust. Casey also allegedly handled documents taken from Jimmy Carter's White House.)

DAVID C. FISCHER, former Special Assistant to the President: Was paid to arrange private meetings between Reagan and wealthy conservative donors to the contras. For his work, he shared hundreds of thousands of dollars with Martin L. Artiano, a one-time Reagan campaign aide.

ROBERT C. McFARLANE, former National Security Adviser: Under investigation for his participation in the Iran-contra affair. (See page 40, The Loyalists–II.)

EDWIN MEESE III, Attorney General: The Senate-House majority's report on the affair in late 1987 suggested Meese had approved a possibly illegal effort to use private funds to ransom U.S. hostages in Lebanon. (See A Meese unto Himself, page 102.)

JONATHAN MILLER, former Deputy Assistant to the President: Resigned in 1987 after being accused of helping move cash to the contras.

LIEUTENANT COLONEL OLIVER L. NORTH, former National Security Council Aide: Fired in 1987 after revelations of his major covert role in diverting to the Contras profits from the sale of U.S. arms to Iran. (See page 37, The Order Taker, and page 38, The Robin Hood [In the Iranian Forest].)

REAR ADMIRAL JOHN M. POINDEXTER, former National Security Adviser: Resigned in 1987 after the President said he discovered the admiral had approved the diversion of funds from the Iranian arms sales to aid the contras. (See page 42, The Government unto Himself, and page 43, The Insulator.)

OTTO J. REICH, U.S. Ambassador to Venezuela: During his previous position as coordinator of the State Department public diplomacy office, Reich awarded more than $400,000 in noncompetitive contracts to International Business Communications, a company tied to North's secret contra support network. Reich has denied the office acted improperly.

III
A MEESE UNTO HIMSELF

EDWIN MEESE III, U.S. Attorney General: Meese, a close
and long-time friend of the President's, has come under fire
many times during his years in the administration. In 1987, he
was being investigated by a special prosecutor for his role in
helping Wedtech Corporation, a scandal-tainted New York
defense contractor. At the same time, another special prosecutor
was investigating his role in the Iran-contra affair, for which
Meese was harshly criticized in the Senate-House majority's
report. The report, issued in November 1987, suggested that
Meese had approved a possibly illegal effort to use private funds
to ransom U.S. hostages in Lebanon. The report also criticized
his performance in conducting an inquiry into the Iran arms
sales in 1986. Meese rejected the criticism as invalid. Meanwhile,
a Senate subcommittee was looking into his apparent failure to
comply with government ethics laws in his 1985 and 1986
financial disclosure forms. During his 1984 confirmation hearings
for attorney general, the then White House counselor was
questioned over his involvement with *Thomas J. Barrack,* a
friend. Barrack arranged the sale of Meese's California house,
took an $83,000 loss on the deal, and then was appointed to a
Department of Interior post (which he later left) after discussing
the appointment with Meese. Another Meese associate, *Edwin
W. Thomas,* in 1981 had made a $15,000 interest-free loan to
Meese's wife, Ursula, and Meese failed to report it on his
financial disclosure form. Thomas then was named to a position
in the San Francisco office of the General Services
Administration; his wife was hired in the Merit System
Protection Board's San Francisco office; and his son was named
to a Labor Department job. An independent counsel's
investigation in 1984 found no criminal violations by Meese on
these and several other allegations of impropriety. (See page 77,
The Presumed Innocent, and page 76, The Witness Against
Himself.)

IV
DOING WELL—BY DOING GOOD?

ROBERT F. BURFORD, Director, Bureau of Land Management, Department of the Interior: Approved regulatory and policy changes that might have enhanced the value of his Colorado ranch and two federal grazing permits held by his three sons. House investigators in 1985 said he broke a formal promise to make no decisions affecting the grazing permits, which he had transferred to his sons after he joined the government in 1981. Burford contended that he had promised to excuse himself only from decisions affecting his family's permits, not grazing permits in general. At the time he signed the rule changes, he said he "owned land but the permits were not in my name."

T. KENNETH CRIBB, JR., Assistant to the President for Domestic Affairs: While in a previous position—a $72,000-a-year Justice Department job—Cribb took six weeks' paid leave to study for his bar exam.

JEAN K. ELDER, Acting Assistant Secretary, Department of Health and Human Services: In 1987, she requested that her nomination as an assistant secretary of HHS be rescinded following charges by Senator Gordon J. Humphrey (R–N.H.) that she had taken official trips to areas near Albion College in Michigan, where her son Paul was playing football between 1983 and 1985.

SHANNON FAIRBANKS, Chief of Staff, Federal Home Loan Bank Board: Sought a $500,000 home loan in 1986 by sending banks mailgrams listing her official title. She said her secretary had mistakenly included her agency affiliation.

DONALD P. HODEL, Secretary of the Interior: While Secretary of Energy, Hodel asked an executive of a utility with extensive dealings with the Department of Energy to help his son and six of his son's friends pay their rock and roll band's touring expenses. Robert H. Short, chief executive of Portland General Electric Company, said he arranged for the band to receive $5,500 of a $34,000 donation the utility had promised Warner Pacific College, where Hodel's son, Dave, had taught. (See page 22, The Optimist.)

DAVID T. KINGSBURY, Assistant Director, National Science Foundation: A House subcommittee in 1987 began an investigation for conflicts of interest stemming from questions about his involvement with a California biotechnology company, IGB Products, which listed Kingsbury as its "founding director" and "scientific adviser." Kingsbury said he had ended relations with the firm before he came to Washington in 1984.

JOHN A. NORRIS, Deputy Commissioner, Food and Drug Administration: Received three noncompetitive consulting contracts from FDA Commissioner Frank E. Young, a former associate, before taking the agency's second highest position. An inspector general's review in 1985 found that Norris had violated no laws but that the agency ignored some rules in making the payments.

CLARENCE M. PENDLETON, JR., Chairman, U.S. Commission on Civil Rights: Turned his part-time position into a full-time job that paid him $67,344 in 1985. This was less than half his income from outside ventures. As former chairman of a federally funded San Diego group that packages loans for the Small Business Administration, Pendleton also has come under investigation by the SBA for helping arrange a contract for his former business partner and special assistant at the commission, Sydney I. Novell, that paid her $77,000 in 1985 in addition to her $41,328 federal salary. Pendleton's lawyer labeled charges of impropriety as baseless.

RICHARD N. PERLE, Assistant Secretary of Defense: Perle recommended in 1982 that the Army consider buying weapons from an Israeli company whose owners had paid him a $50,000 consulting fee a year earlier, shortly before he joined the government. In 1986, he was the subject of an internal Pentagon inquiry over the auction of a novel he proposed to write based on his running feud with an assistant secretary of state during Reagan's first term. Bidding for the book passed $300,000 before Perle said he would drop negotiations with publishers, citing the possibility of an "appearance of impropriety."

THOMAS M. ROBERTS, Commissioner, Nuclear Regulatory Commission: Told a House subcommittee in 1987 that in 1985, against a U.S. attorney's advice, he met with a lawyer for a nuclear power plant that was under federal criminal investigation. He said he did not believe the meeting was improper. Roberts also has come under fire for allegedly mishandling an investigation of a leaked NRC document. The document apparently went from his office to the files of a Louisiana utility. Roberts denied any impropriety, but six congressional chairmen urged him to resign because of the incident. (See pages 54–56, The Foxes Who Guarded the Chicken Coops VI and VII.)

TERRENCE M. SCANLON, Chairman, Consumer Product Safety Commission: Lawmakers and officials during 1987 hearings by a House subcommittee charged that Scanlon had slowed action against dangerous products, including all-terrain vehicles; resolved ambiguous statutes against the consumer; and let "infighting" bring the agency near paralysis. In response, legislation was introduced late in 1987 to limit the power of the agency's chairman. In 1986 Scanlon was cleared by the Justice Department of charges that he misused his office. Allegations included that he had used agency employees for personal typing and anti-abortion activities.

FAITH RYAN WHITTLESEY, Ambassador to Switzerland: Whittlesey raised an $80,000 embassy fund from private donors and hired the son of one donor to a $62,400-a-year job at the Bern embassy. In 1986, Attorney General Edwin Meese III decided not to seek an independent counsel to investigate whether she had improperly assisted major donors to the fund. The department later refused to turn over to the Senate Judiciary Committee an internal staff report recommending that an independent counsel be named to investigate Whittlesey. The Whittlesey case forced Secretary of State George P. Shultz to call for a ban on future solicitation and the use of privately donated funds to cover embassy expenses such as entertaining. (See page 35, The Fabulists–IV.)

CHARLES Z. WICK, Director, U.S. Information Agency: Taped conversations with public officials without their permission. He apologized in 1984 for invading the privacy of his callers. He installed a $32,000 security system at his Washington home at taxpayer expense, then repaid $22,000 of it after White House criticism, along with $4,436 for personal calls on two telephones that had been installed in his home at government expense. He also accepted responsibility for USIA's hiring of a number of friends and relatives of top administration officials. In 1987, Wick acknowledged that USIA's use of a $175-a-day consultant on youth affairs while the consultant was lobbying for an agency grant for his organization was a "blatant conflict of interest." But, the director added, "That doesn't necessarily mean there can't be a benefit to the agency . . ." The consultant subsequently resigned, saying he did not see a conflict in his dual roles but wanted to avoid congressional criticism. (See page 34, The Fabulists–III; page 61, The Democracy Projector; page 65, The Folks Who Don't Have a Bigoted Bone in Their Bodies–II; and page 62, The Tapeworm.)

JOSEPH R. WRIGHT, Deputy Director, Office of Management and Budget: Contacted a senior Energy Department official about a case against an Oklahoma oil company in which Wright owned more than $250,000 in stock. The department delayed its case against the company, which was run by Wright's father, for more than two years. Wright said he had sought no special treatment.

V
Epitaphs for the Gone-But-Not-to-Be-Forgotten

RICHARD V. ALLEN, National Security Adviser: Resigned in 1981 amid controversy over a $1,000 "honorarium" and three watches given by a Japanese reporter who had asked his help in arranging an interview with Nancy Reagan. He said he forgot to report the gift but hadn't meant to keep it. (See page 35, The Fabulists–IV.)

THORNE G. AUCHTER, Assistant Secretary, Occupational Safety and Health Administration: In 1981, Auchter approved the dismissal of $12,680 in penalties and twelve proposed safety citations for a Kansas company whose parent firm later named him president. Auchter resigned to join the firm in 1984. An agency review found no improper conduct.

JAMES M. BEGGS, Chief Administrator, National Aeronautics and Space Administration: Was indicted in 1985 on charges that he defrauded the government while he was an executive at General Dynamics Corporation. The charges involved the fraudulent hiding of cost overruns on an Army contract to develop the DIVAD antiaircraft gun. The Justice Department dropped the charges in 1987, admitting its theory of prosecution was wrong. He took a leave of absence following the charges and resigned in 1986.

DANIEL K. BENJAMIN, Chief of Staff, Department of Labor: Resigned in 1984 after it was disclosed that he had been given free use of a sailboat owned by a lobbyist for a trade association that deals with the department. A departmental review found no conflict of interest.

DONALD P. BOGARD, President, Legal Services Corporation: Was criticized for receiving a contract negotiated by William F. Harvey, then LSC chairman, that included membership in a private club, one year's severance pay if he were fired, and two government-paid trips a month to his Indianapolis home. A federal audit found no impropriety.

WILLIAM F. BOLGER, Postmaster General: Participated in postal-rate deliberations while negotiating a possible job with a mass-mailing group whose members would have been affected by the rate changes. Shortly before resigning in 1984, he named the wife of a retiring postal official and close friend to a postmaster's job in the Cape Cod town where the couple had purchased a retirement home.

CHARLES M. BUTLER III, Chairman, Federal Energy Regulatory Commission: Refused to disqualify himself from new agency cases involving clients that he or his associates had represented in his Houston law firm.

EDGAR F. CALLAHAN, Chairman, National Credit Union Administration: Improperly billed the government for $21,250 in moving and living expenses. He was ordered to repay it.

CARLOS C. CAMPBELL, Assistant Secretary, Economic Development Administration: Resigned in 1983 after it was disclosed that he helped arrange a grant to an institute run by a longtime acquaintance. The institute enrolled him in a $24,000 computer course at no cost and provided him with a free home computer. He denied any conflict and said certain congressmen had wanted his ouster for opposing pork barrel projects.

JOSEPH CANZERI, Deputy Assistant to the President and Assistant to the Deputy Chief of Staff: Resigned in 1982 after it was disclosed that he had accepted below-market financing from Laurence S. Rockefeller and a California developer for a $380,000 Georgetown townhouse. He also acknowledged double-billing the White House and the Republican National Committee for travel expenses, but said the double billings were not intended.

MICHAEL CARDENAS, Administrator, Small Business Administration: Was asked by the White House in 1982 to resign after complaints about his performance and concern about internal investigations into conflict-of-interest charges involving SBA contracts.

GERALD P. CARMEN, Ambassador, European Office of the United Nations, Geneva: While an administrator of the General Services Administration from 1981 to 1984, Carmen failed to list a $425,000 low-interest government loan on a financial disclosure form and allegedly placed family members and friends in government jobs. The administration followed up on this by sending him to Geneva.

MICHAEL J. CONNOLLY, General Counsel, Equal Employment Opportunity Commission: Resigned in 1982 amid allegations he conspired to end an EEOC investigation of a company represented by his brother.

DONALD J. DEVINE, Director, Office of Personnel Management: Withdrew his nomination in 1985 for a second four-year term after a Senate witness accused him of lying. Acting OPM director Loretta Cornelius testified that Devine asked her to falsely claim that she knew about an arrangement in which he had signed an order giving himself full power to run the office while, technically, he was serving as her assistant.

BETTY LOU DOTSON, Director, Office of Civil Rights, Department of Health and Human Services: Forced to resign in 1987 during a federal investigation into her travel expenses and contracting practices. In five years of office, she took 126 trips to 38 places at a cost of $86,868 and ran up an additional $6,840 in taxi fares. Several trips made abroad at government expense had nothing to do with HHS, she had said, but she was representing the Reagan administration.

ROSSLEE GREEN DOUGLAS, Director, Office of Minority Impact, Department of Energy: Resigned in 1986 while under investigation by the General Accounting Office on charges that she took government-paid trips to her home state not directly related to her program and trips to vacation spots at government expense in which she stayed longer than required to complete her official duties.

CLARENCE DUFFY, Human Rights Commission member, U.S. Postal Service, Dubuque, Iowa: Resigned in 1984 over his reference to female postal workers as "stupid broads."

HERBERT E. ELLINGWOOD, White House aide: While chairman of the Merit Systems Protection Board, Ellingwood was widely criticized for suggesting that an evangelical Christian group start what became known as a "Christian talent bank" for federal appointments. Ellingwood, a long-time friend of *Edwin Meese III,* also was accused by a House subcommittee of arranging a Merit Board job for Gretchen Thomas, the wife of mutual friend *Edwin W. Thomas,* who had given Meese's wife a $15,000 no-interest loan. Meese hired Ellingwood for a Justice Department post that required no Senate confirmation. Ellingwood resigned in 1986 to work for Reverend Pat Robertson's presidential campaign.

JOHN M. FEDDERS, Director, Division of Enforcement, Securities and Exchange Commission: Resigned in 1985 after his wife, Charlotte, testified in divorce proceedings that he repeatedly beat her and ran up huge debts during their eighteen-year marriage.

GUY W. FISKE, Deputy Secretary, Department of Commerce: Resigned in 1983 after it was disclosed that he had talked with Communications Satellite Corporation about a possible job at the same time he was in charge of a proposed sale of U.S. weather satellites to the firm. The Justice Department declined to bring charges.

MARY ANN GILLEECE, Deputy Under Secretary for Procurement, Department of Defense: Resigned in 1985 after the Pentagon's inspector general found she had violated ethics rules in writing letters to twenty-eight defense contractors seeking a $30,000 retainer for a consulting firm she and an aide planned to form when she left the government.

LOUIS O. GIUFFRIDA, Director, Federal Emergency Management Agency: Resigned in 1985, the day before a House subcommittee issued its report on accusations that he improperly intervened in agency awards and that he should repay $5,091 for federally funded trips to Europe and Mexico by his wife. Giuffrida also had attended a $250-a-plate reception for Vice President George Bush as the guest of a FEMA contractor, which later billed the agency for the ticket and for Giuffrida's attendance at a dinner honoring President Reagan. (See page 7, The Confidence Man.)

EDWIN J. GRAY, Chairman, Federal Home Loan Bank Board: Repaid some $26,000 in travel costs for himself and his wife. He also spent $47,254 to renovate his office and reception area. In 1986, he apologized to Congress for permitting large amounts of his and other bank board officials' travel and personal expenses to be paid by thrift organizations. His term expired in 1987. (See page 10, The Economizers–III.)

ARTHUR HULL HAYES, JR., Commissioner, Food and Drug Administration: Resigned in 1983 after allegations that he collected expenses both from the government and from a private group he addressed while on an official trip. The Justice Department declined to bring charges.

WILLIAM S. HEFFELFINGER, Assistant Secretary, Department of Energy: Accused of falsifying his resume, deceiving federal investigators, and violating civil service merit protection regulations. He resigned in 1982.

J. LYNN HELMS, Administrator, Federal Aviation Administration: Resigned in 1984 when grand juries investigated his earlier business dealings. News reports said that over eight years, he and an associate had "bled dry" businesses they had acquired by shifting funds from one to another. The businesses also were reported to have several million dollars in government-guaranteed debts. After he resigned, Justice Department investigations dissolved.

DENNIS E. LeBLANC, Associate Administrator, Department of Commerce: LeBlanc, who had been Reagan's bodyguard while he was governor of California, in his $58,000-a-year Commerce job spent part of his time chopping wood and sweeping out the barn at President Reagan's Santa Barbara ranch.

JOHN McELDERRY, Denver regional administrator, Department of Health and Human Services: Resigned after charges he used his federal position to promote and sell Amway products.

JOHN R. McKEAN, Chairman, U.S. Postal Service Board of Governors: Arranged $118,000 in loans for Edwin Meese III, then White House counselor, and for White House aide Michael K. Deaver in 1981. Both men later recommended McKean for the postal service job. An independent counsel's probe of Meese found no connection between the financial assistance by McKean, *Thomas J. Barrack,* and *Edwin W. Thomas* (see page 102, A Meese unto Himself) and their subsequent federal jobs. In 1986, allegations were being examined that McKean participated in the award of a $300,000 Postal Service contract to a San Francisco law firm for which he had done accounting work. The General Accounting Office found that it appeared McKean had used his position to influence the postmaster general's awarding of the contract.

ROBERT P. NIMMO, Administrator, Veterans Administration: Resigned in 1982 before a General Accounting Office report criticized him for such things as improper use of chartered military aircraft and first-class airline service. He also was forced to repay the government $6,641 for improper use of a chauffeur-driven automobile. (See page 9, The Economizers–II.)

ROSLYN PAYNE, Chief Executive Officer and President, Federal Asset Disposition Association: Resigned in 1987 as chief executive of the quasi-government company that manages and sells property the government inherited from failed savings and loans. But Payne retained her $250,000-a-year salary and title as president. Her resignation came during congressional hearings into allegations of mismanagement and potential conflicts of interest.

DR. WESLEY A. PLUMMER, Director of Civil Rights, Department of Transportation: Resigned in 1983 during an investigation into his using government secretaries and postage for soliciting funds from department contractors on behalf of a private organization he headed.

NORMAN H. RAIDEN, General Counsel, Federal Home Loan Bank Board: A congressional oversight committee in 1986 said Raiden, who resigned in 1985, had violated federal conflict-of-interest laws by signing documents that affected a California savings and loan that he once had represented as its leading outside lawyer. The charges grew out of a House subcommittee's inquiry into the failure in April 1985 of The Beverly Hills Savings and Loan Association. Raiden acknowledged during the subcommittee's hearings that he had signed at least nine documents related to the thrift. But he said none of the documents involved issues he had handled as an attorney in a Los Angeles law firm. After resigning his federal post he returned to the same law firm.

EVERETT G. RANK, Administrator Agricultural Stabilization and Conservation Service, Department of Agriculture: Designed and administered the 1983 payment-in-kind (PIK) program that later provided his farm with more than $1 million in free federal cotton. Rank said he did not know that his partners had enrolled the California farm in the program. The Justice Department in 1985 decided there were no grounds to prosecute him, but said USDA should see that Rank didn't violate conflict-of-interest law in the future.

ALFRED S. REGNERY, Administrator Office of Juvenile Justice and Delinquency Prevention, Department of Justice: Approved a grant proposal for a book on juvenile justice that included a provision under which he would be paid $1,000 to write a chapter.

ARMAND REISER, Special Assistant to the Secretary of Energy: Resigned in 1981 after it was reported that he failed to disclose $106,840 in earnings from five energy-related companies on the financial report he was required to file under the federal ethics law. He subsequently reported the income in the face of inquiries by House investigators, but he said his resignation was not related to the episode.

ISIDORO RODRIGUEZ, Director, Office of Minority Affairs, Department of Agriculture: Fired in 1983 after writing a memo calling for the relaxation of federal civil rights enforcement. He also was reported to have collected unemployment benefits while working as a government consultant before receiving his federal appointment.

ROBERT A. ROWLAND, Assistant Secretary, Occupational Safety and Health Administration: Resigned in 1985 after being criticized for participating in agency decisions that could have affected companies in which he owned more than $1 million in stock. He had been involved in decisions not to enact tighter rules for formaldehyde, benzene, and ethylene oxide while he had stock in companies including Tenneco, Exxon, Eastman Kodak, and Monsanto—firms that use such products. A federal review found Rowland had been granted a conflict-of-interest waiver by then Labor Secretary Raymond J. Donovan.

RET. ADMIRAL HAROLD E. SHEAR, Administrator, Maritime Administration: Approved a ship-repair plan that provided $2.1 million to a naval architecture firm whose chairman owns the steamship firm that formerly employed Shear. Shear had received a $45,000 severance payment from the company when he resigned after eight months of service to join the government in 1981. A federal review concluded he had inadvertently erred in not properly reporting the payment on his financial disclosure form.

VICTOR A. SCHROEDER, Director and President, U.S. Synthetic Fuels Corporation: Resigned in 1983 after disclosures that he had offered another director help with his private business in return for supporting a Schroeder proposal. It also was disclosed that he had awarded noncompetitive contracts to former business associates. (See page 85, The Victors–I.)

WILLIAM FRENCH SMITH, Attorney General: While head of the department that, among other duties, prosecutes tax-code violations, Smith invested in a tax shelter that would have brought him $66,000 in deductions—four times his investment—although the Internal Revenue Service frowns on such shelters. He later agreed to forgo the deductions. Shortly before taking office in 1981, he accepted a $50,000 severance payment from a California steel company of which he had been a director for six years. After disclosure of the payment, he returned it. In 1982, the Justice Department closed its investigation and said no further probe was needed. He also repaid $11,000 for improper use of a government limousine by his wife.

NANCY HARVEY STEORTS, Chairman, Consumer Product Safety Commission: Used her government driver to take her to the hairdresser, to pick up dresses at a store, and for other personal errands. She also ordered the driver, who earned $14,000 a year, to buy a suit and spent $8,000 to $10,000 in government funds to redecorate her office.

VICTOR M. THOMPSON, JR., President, U.S. Synthetic Fuels Corporation: Resigned in 1984 after an internal review said he violated ethics rules in voting on decisions involving government funds for a Texas oilman whose help he had sought to shore up his private business. (See page 87, The Victors–II.)

NORMAN TURE, Under Secretary for Tax and Economic Affairs, Department of the Treasury: While in office in 1981, Ture helped to arrange a $230,000 contract for an economic forecasting model he had developed and partly owned. An inspector general's inquiry found that Ture, who was selling his interest in the model for $60,000, had at most committed a technical violation of federal rules.

LEONARD VANCE, Director, Health Standards Programs, Occupational Safety and Health Administration: In 1984, a congressional subcommittee asked Vance to provide four log books after it had received internal OSHA documents indicating that Vance had blocked efforts to restrict the use of ethylene oxide, a carcinogen used by hospitals, after meeting privately with a top manufacturer of the chemical. The subcommittee asked him to provide four log books. Vance refused, saying they were personal property, but faced with mounting congressional pressure, he agreed to comply. Then he said three of the four log books were missing because his dogs had been sick and vomited on them.

FRED J. VILLELLA, Executive Deputy Director, Federal Emergency Management Agency: Resigned in 1984 following allegations that he had more than $70,000 in renovations made to transform part of a dormitory at an agency training center in Maryland into a residence. He also was accused of misappropriating more than $160,000 in government funds, of using employees for personal errands, and of sexually harassing an aide.

W. LAWRENCE WALLACE, Assistant Attorney General: Resigned in 1986 after his personal finances came under investigation by a separate independent counsel. Wallace had failed to file his personal income tax return for two years. The independent counsel late in 1987 found no basis for prosecution, saying Wallace had committed a "technical violation" of a law that makes it a misdemeanor to fail to file tax returns. However, the counsel said, Wallace filed the returns after learning they were due and that he was owed a refund for those years.

ROBERT E. WATKINS, Deputy Assistant Secretary for Automotive Affairs, Department of Commerce: Resigned in 1987 after disclosure that he had solicited Japanese car manufacturers to hire him to form a trade association to represent their interests against "protectionist and xenophobic" U.S. policies. The chairman of the House subcommittee that began investigating him said that at the same time Watkins was sending out resumes, he was representing the U.S. government as a trade negotiator with Japan and Canada.

JAMES G. WATT, Secretary of the Interior: Resigned in 1983 during an uproar over his remark that he had an advisory panel with "a black, . . . a woman, two Jews and a cripple." In 1981 he used a National Park Service fund to finance two private Christmas parties at Arlington Cemetery's Custis-Lee Mansion. (See page 70, The Folks Who Don't Have a Bigoted Bone in Their Bodies–V, and page 90, The Prophets–II.)

WILLIAM A. WILSON, Ambassador to the Vatican: Wilson, one of Reagan's closest friends, was forced to resign in 1986 after disclosure of unusual unauthorized dealings with Libya including a secret meeting in 1985 with Libyan leader Moammar Gadhafi. In 1984, it was learned that he had retained posts on the boards of two corporations when he became ambassador. This was considered an unusual exception to State Department policy.

VI
Environmental Losses

PETER N. BIBKO, Philadelphia Regional Administrator, Environmental Protection Agency: Was dismissed in 1983 after investigators found he took questionable sick leave, frequently was driven by government chauffeur between Washington and Philadelphia, and charged the agency for personal telephone calls.

ANNE GORSUCH BURFORD, Administrator, EPA: Resigned in 1983 after a confrontation with Congress over withheld documents and charges of mismanagement and political manipulation of agency programs. She was accused of delaying a toxic waste cleanup grant to California so as not to help the Democratic Senate campaign of then Governor Edmund G. (Jerry) Brown, Jr., and of indicating to a New Mexico refinery that it might not be prosecuted if it failed to meet EPA lead standards.

LOUIS J. CORDIA, Deputy Chief of Federal Activities, EPA: Resigned in 1983 after it was disclosed that he had compiled a "hit list" of agency employees to be hired, fired, or promoted because of their political leanings.

ROBERT FUNKHOUSER, Director, Office of International Activities: Resigned in 1983 after allegations that he helped Dow Chemical Company influence international trade talks on toxic chemicals.

JOHN W. HERNANDEZ, JR., Deputy Administrator, EPA: Resigned in 1983 after his staff disclosed that he allowed Dow Chemical to review a report naming it a dioxin polluter. He was said to have pressured agency officials to tone down the report.

JOHN P. HORTON, Assistant Administrator, EPA: Resigned in 1983 after allegations that he used government employees for private business on government time.

MATTHEW N. NOVICK, Inspector General, EPA: Resigned in 1983 after allegations he used government employees for private business and mishandled agency investigations.

THEODORE B. OLSON, Assistant Attorney General: In 1986, Olson came under a lengthy investigation by an independent counsel over charges that he gave false testimony to Congress in 1983 about the administration's withholding of EPA documents. Olson has denied the charges.

ROBERT M. PERRY, General Counsel, EPA: Was investigated for possible perjury for telling Congress that he was not familiar with books containing information, much of it derogatory, about his subordinates. He also testified that he did not sign an EPA settlement agreement with a subsidiary of his former employer, Exxon, despite evidence that he had.

JAMES W. SANDERSON, part-time EPA consultant: His 1983 nomination as EPA assistant administrator was withdrawn after disclosure that he had represented companies regulated by EPA while consulting for the agency. He denied there was any conflict of interest.

JOHN A. TODHUNTER, Assistant Administrator, EPA: Resigned in 1983 after allegations that he held private meetings with chemical lobbyists that unduly influenced him before he decided not to regulate formaldehyde and other toxic substances. He denied the allegations.

VII
Housecleaning in Housing and Urban Development

JAMES C. CUMMINGS, Deputy Assistant Secretary, Department of Housing and Urban Development: While HUD's Chicago regional chief, Cummings rented an apartment at bargain rates from a friend who did business with the agency.

DICK EUDALY, Regional Administrator, Fort Worth, Texas, Field Office, HUD: Resigned in 1984 following allegations that he demoted or transferred five subordinates who questioned his efforts to manipulate an agency program so two Texas cities could receive grants.

JAYNE H. GALLAGHER, Director, Office of Public Affairs, HUD: Failed in 1984 and 1985 financial disclosure forms to report more than $300,000 in debts incurred when she and two business partners defaulted on more than $1 million in federal and New York state loans. HUD Secretary Samuel R. Pierce, Jr., declined to take action against her.

DuBOIS L. GILLIAM, Deputy Assistant Secretary, HUD: Resigned in 1987 while under investigation by the Justice Department about the misuse of a $600,000 community development grant he approved for a Virgin Islands company, Crown Bay Local Development Corporation. People affiliated with Crown Bay paid for three trips to St. Thomas by Gilliam and his family.

DONALD I. HOVDE, Under Secretary, HUD: Repaid the government $3,100 for improperly using a government car and driver for commuting and to chauffeur his wife, neighbors, and parents on various excursions. He also took trips to Puerto Rico and Italy paid for by builders and realtors. (See page 10, The Economizers–III.)

DANIEL M. HUGHES, Deputy Under Secretary, HUD: Over the objections of HUD's career staff, Hughes urged HUD officials to approve an Urban Development Action Grant involving his new development firm. The grant was awarded in 1984.

EMANUEL SAVAS, Assistant Secretary, HUD: Resigned in 1983 after charges he'd used HUD staff to write and edit his aptly titled book, *Privatizing the Public Sector.* He also charged the government for twenty weekend trips to the New York area, where he stayed at home. Savas appointed a panel that awarded a HUD contract to a firm that had paid him $33,000 in consulting fees.

BILL J. SLOAN, Regional Administrator, San Francisco Field Office, HUD: Resigned in 1984 after repaying $6,800 he had billed the government in improper travel expenses. (See p. 8, The Economizers–I)

BAKER ARMSTRONG SMITH, Assistant to the Secretary for Labor Relations, HUD: Resigned in 1983 after allegations that he had curbed HUD's enforcement program, improperly dismissed employees because of their union backgrounds, and had his secretary type his master's thesis and mail Christmas gifts.

WAYNE E. TANGYE, Supervisor in Reno, Nevada, HUD: Tangye, an aide to Sloan, resigned in 1984 after investigators ound he had charged the agency $12,000 in improper travel expenses. The agency attached his paycheck and pension.

GORDON D. WALKER, Deputy Under Secretary, HUD: Resigned in 1986 during an investigation by HUD's inspector general. While working for the government, Walker also earned at least $80,000 speaking and writing for a group that sells books and tapes on how to make money in real estate. He also had lectured for the group while on HUD trips.

VIII
Some Who Didn't Make It

WILLIAM M. BELL: Withdrew his nomination as chairman of the Equal Employment Opportunity Commission in 1982 after it was disclosed that his one-man Detroit job recruitment firm was not listed in the phone book and that he had not placed anyone in a job in the previous year.

HENRY Y. CHAVIRA: Withdrew as a nominee to the Legal Services Corporation in 1983 after it was disclosed that he had been arrested on a larceny charge and that his ex-wife was pursuing him for delinquent child-support payments.

JUDGE DOUGLAS H. GINSBURG: Withdrew as a nominee to the Supreme Court justice in 1987, following the Senate's rejection of Circuit Judge Robert J. Bork, because of disclosures that he had smoked marijuana. The pot-smoking ruckus obscured the debate about his qualifications. Just a year before, when Ginsburg was named to his federal appeals court judgeship, the American Bar Association rated him barely qualified. In addition, serious ethical questions had been raised over his performance as a Justice Department lawyer handling a cable television case and cable regulations matters while he held a $140,000 investment in a cable company. Late in 1987, the Justice Department began a formal preliminary investigation of whether an independent counsel should be appointed to look into the allegations of conflict of interest in the cable television cases.

REVEREND B. SAM HART: Reagan withdrew Hart's nomination to the Commission on Civil Rights in 1982 after reports that he owed back taxes and rent in connection with his Philadelphia radio station. It also was disclosed that he had defaulted on a federal small business loan and was delinquent on a state loan repayment.

ERNEST LEFEVER: Withdrew in 1981 as a nominee for Assistant Secretary of State for Human Rights after a Senate committee recommended against his confirmation. The committee heard testimony that Lefever's conservative foundation had distributed material promoting infant formula to Third World mothers after taking a $25,000 donation from Nestle, a major infant-formula maker. His defeat primarily was due to controversy about his commitment to human rights. (See page 32, The Fabulists–II, and page 49, The Foxes Who Guarded the Chicken Coops–II.)

LESLIE LENKOWSKY: Was nominated to be deputy director of the U.S. Information Agency but was rejected by the Senate Foreign Relations Committee in 1984 after several senators accused him of lying to the panel about his role in blacklisting people, including Walter Cronkite and Coretta Scott King, from the agency's overseas speaking program. Other witnesses testified that he was instrumental in compiling a blacklist of speakers too liberal to speak for the agency, which Lenkowsky denied under oath.

GLENN C. LOURY: Loury, a professor at Harvard University's John F. Kennedy School of Government, was Reagan's choice for Under Secretary of Education. In June 1987, he unexpectedly withdrew his name from consideration for the post, citing "personal reasons." Days before, he had been charged with assaulting a twenty-three-year-old Boston woman, Pamela Foster. He entered a plea of not guilty; Foster later

ropped the charges. Later in 1987, he was charged with
possession of cocaine and marijuana. He pleaded not guilty.

**JAMES L. MALONE,Assistant Secretary, Department of
State:** In 1986, the protégé of Senator Jesse Helms (R–N.C.)
became the first ambassadorial nominee ever rejected by the
Senate Foreign Relations Committee. Before turning him down
as ambassador to Belize, senators charged that Malone had lied
to the committee and violated a pledge that, while serving as an
assistant secrtary of state, he would not deal with Japan, West
Germany, and Taiwan, where he had previously represented
clients.

WILLIAM E. McCANN: Was announced as the nominee for
ambassadorship to Ireland but his name was withdrawn in 1981
after it was reported that his insurance company was under
investigation by New York authorities for selling insurance
without a license and because of allegations that he had business
ties to a convicted swindler. McCann was not individually
accused; he said the allegations were unfounded.

ROBERT N. MILLER, U.S. Attorney in Colorado: In 1984,
Miller had been reprimanded by then Attorney General William
French Smith for his handling of a federal bid-rigging case and
his comments to reporters about it. In 1987, he was nominated
for a U.S. District Court judgeship. During a grueling, two-hour
hearing before the Senate Judiciary Committee, he was asked
why, in response to a Senate questionnaire, he had failed to
mention the reprimand by Smith. The question was whether he
had ever been "disciplined for professional misconduct." Miller
told the committee he did not consider the Smith reprimand
"official." Early in 1988, he asked the President to withdraw his
nomination.

ROBERT E. RADER, JR.: Nominated to the Occupational
Safety and Health Review Committee. He had been ordered by a
federal judge in 1985 to pay a $3,000 fine for misrepresenting
facts and failing to comply with code orders in a race
discrimination suit. He also was reported to have advised

corporate clients to resist OSHA workplace inspections. The nomination was killed in committee in 1986.

WARREN RICHARDSON: Withdrew as a nominee for Assistant Secretary of Health and Human Services in 1981 after complaints about his alleged antisemitism and disclosures that he had been a lobbyist for the Liberty Lobby, which critics have called a racist organization.

JEFFERSON B. SESSIONS III, U.S. Attorney in Alabama: As nominee for a federal judgeship in 1986, Sessions ran into trouble in the Senate Judiciary Committee when witnesses said he called the National Association for the Advancement of Colored People and the American Civil Liberties Union "un-American" and "communist inspired" and said he had made racially insensitive remarks. Sessions said his remarks were misinterpreted or out of context; the nomination was rejected. (See page 67, The Folks Who Don't Have a Bigoted Bone in Their Bodies–III.)

E. DONALD SHAPIRO: Withdrew as a nominee to the Legal Services Corporation in 1983 after reports that he had been investigated for allegations of improperly enriching himself as dean of a New York law school. The investigation later was dropped.

SHERMAN E. UNGER, General Counsel, Department of Commerce: Died in 1983, before action on his nomination for a federal judgeship. The nomination had been made despite the American Bar Association's finding that he lacked personal integrity and had lied to the ABA. He was accused of unethical courtroom maneuvers, tax avoidance, and fraud.

All of the foregoing entries are based on reports in the press, most importantly the *Washington Post,* **the** *New York Times,* **and the** *Wall Street Journal.*

President Ron's Pursuit
of Excellence–II

*[A reporter] Question: "If you were truly unaware
of the millions of dollars in government money
and government operations that [Lt. Col. Oliver]
North and [Adm. John M.] Poindexter were
directing to the contras, what does this say about
your management style?*

*"You have said in your speech that your
management style in the contra-Iran affair [sic]
does* not match your previous track record. The
Tower board criticized your management style.

"If you were unaware of these things and
forgot when you actually approved the Iranian
arms sale, what does it say about the way you've
been managing the presidency?"

*"I've been reading a great deal about my
management style. I think that most people in
business will agree that it is a proper
management style. You get the best people you
can to do a job. Then you don't hang over their
shoulder criticizing everything they do or picking
at them on how they're doing it. You set the
policy, and I set the policy in this administration.
And they are then to implement it."*

—News conference March 19, 1987

"IT'S AWFUL THAT SO MANY PEOPLE AROUND THE PRESIDENT DID THESE THINGS — WHO IN THE WORLD HIRED THOSE PEOPLE?"

©1987 HERBLOCK

From *Herblock at Large*, Pantheon Books, 1987.

If you would like to order additional copies of *PRESIDENT RON'S APPOINTMENT BOOK* or *QUOTATIONS FROM PRESIDENT RON*, please complete this form.

Please send me:

_____ copies of *PRESIDENT RON'S APPOINTMENT BOOK* (01663-8)
$4.95 per copy

_____ copies of *QUOTATIONS FROM PRESIDENT RON* (00925-9)
$4.95 per copy